# RADICAL HUMILITY

"*Radical Humility* is a game-changing book that redefines leadership in the modern world. Through the lens of cooperative relationships, Urs Koenig emphasizes the power of self-knowledge, strong relationships, and a growth mindset to achieve remarkable results. With practical insights and a refreshing perspective, this book is a must-read for leaders at all levels, offering a clear road map to cultivate the kind of humility that revolutionizes not only our work and professional relationships but also our lives and world."

—DR. MARSHALL GOLDSMITH, Thinkers50 #1 Executive Coach and *New York Times* bestselling author of *The Earned Life*, *Triggers*, and *What Got You Here Won't Get You There*

"Confidence and humility aren't opposites. They're complements. With *Radical Humility*, Urs Koenig has created the ultimate playbook for turning one of our most misunderstood character traits into a leadership superpower."

—DANIEL H. PINK, #1 *New York Times* bestselling author of *Drive* and *The Power of Regret*

"This remarkable book has it all: engaging stories (some with gripping suspense), powerful insights, and practical advice. It is by far my favorite book on leadership this year, managing to be research based, personal, and wise all at once. Its author clearly models that which he advocates, and if we, his readers, can do likewise, the world will be a better place."

—AMY C. EDMONDSON, Novartis Professor of Leadership and Management, Harvard Business School, and author of *Right Kind of Wrong*

"Urs Koenig understands that we need to move beyond old-school ideas of leadership to meet today's challenges. He not only offers a compelling vision—one that meets the demands of a diverse, dynamic, and rapidly changing workforce—but also offers clear guidance on how to get there. This book is filled with insightful and practical ideas that can foster a new era of compassionate, empathetic, and purpose-driven leaders. *Radical Humility* will help you unleash the power of teams and organizations. It's a book you will want to read twice then slip under your boss's door."

—**HUBERT JOLY**, former CEO, Best Buy; senior lecturer, Harvard Business School; and author of *The Heart of Business*

"*Radical Humility* is more than a book. It's a movement toward a more humble, more empathetic, and—ultimately—more effective leadership style. For anyone looking to navigate the challenges of leadership in the twenty-first century, this book is an indispensable guide."

—**GREG MCKEOWN**, *New York Times* bestselling author of *Essentialism* and *Effortless*; host of *The Greg McKeown Podcast*

"No one party or person has a monopoly on good ideas. The best leaders are humble enough to welcome wisdom from a variety of sources. Urs Koenig understands that and in *Radical Humility* reveals the underestimated power of humility as a leadership tool."

—**DEVAL PATRICK**, former Massachusetts governor; professor, Harvard Kennedy School of Government

"As chairman of The Ritz-Carlton Hotel Company, humility was one of the most powerful secrets to always stay ahead of the curve by creating the most successful brand extensions in the hospitality industry. Practicing the Five Shifts framework and dozens of actionable insights on leadership outlined in *Radical Humility* will put you and your team on the path to prosperity and a healthy corporate culture of positivity and empowerment."

—**HERVÉ J.L. HUMLER**, chairman emeritus, The Ritz-Carlton Hotel Company LLC

"Leadership and achievement have evolved radically for this generation—far less command-and-control and far more flexibility, self-awareness, and transparency. *Radical Humility* is a must-read for this new kind of leader."

—**ASHEESH ADVANI,** CEO, JA (Junior Achievement) Worldwide

"Conventional wisdom equates strength with being stoic, decisive, and invulnerable—to appear resilient and unaffected by the day-to-day swirl that surrounds us. *Radical Humility* reveals the true strength of leadership—humility. Displaying humility demonstrates that we are all a work in progress. It enables leaders to take ownership of unpopular decisions, accept responsibility for mistakes or failures, and create a safe environment where these things are both expected and accepted. In the end, it helps us all become a better version of ourselves and leads to individual and organizational success."

—**BRAD D. SMITH,** president, Marshall University, and former CEO, Intuit

"Without humility, I never would have become the best version of myself as an NFL player, a leader of men, and a person. Urs Koenig's book is essential reading for leaders of all stripes."

—**MERRIL HOGE,** author of *Find a Way* and *Brainwashed*

"*Radical Humility* expands on some core humble leadership ideas with Urs Koenig's unique emphasis, based upon illuminating real-world experiences. It is wonderfully researched and integrated, including an interactive dimension to get readers engaged with the concept, and it presents a broad framework for people to work within. As is the author's experience (reinforced by the wisdom of other key military, commercial, and academic thought leaders), humble leadership is not about vulnerability, avoidance, or deferral. It is about superior information gathering—and influence—to drive better decisions. With "radical," humility and action are fused in a way that will inspire many leaders to be more proactive, more engaging, and more committed to leading with humility based on openness and trust."

—**PETER SCHEIN,** coauthor of *Humble Leadership*

"Military is a 'people business.' It is therefore not surprising that leadership is one of the most important competencies for armed forces. After reading his book, it became clear to me that Urs Koenig's concepts on leadership are also relevant to armed forces. He is passionate about applying what he has learned to become a better leader, just as I strive to be every day. The reflections on decades of experience, summarized in a practical manual, make *Radical Humility* a stimulating read that I can recommend to anyone who wants to develop their own leadership skills."

—LT. GEN. THOMAS SÜSSLI, chief of the Swiss Armed Forces

"So much has been written about leadership that it is hard to identify the books that are the real gems on the subject. *Radical Humility* is one of those gems. It's a complete guide to being a humble and effective leader in today's complex world. It stands out as a valuable resource for anyone in authority who desires to form meaningful relationships and build top-performing teams that deliver impressive results. The book is filled with insights, actionable advice, and real-life examples that illustrate how leading with humility is crucial to leading successfully. *Radical Humility* is destined to become a classic favorite among those who want to lead well."

—HOLLY WESCHE, owner and CEO, Wesche Jewelers, and former board chair, Jewelers of America

"A must-read for anyone seeking the right kind of framework on leadership in today's complex world. *Radical Humility* is designed to give valuable knowledge and a path to implement this knowledge in discrete, useful steps. Peter Drucker, the father of modern management, once wrote: 'We spend too much time teaching leaders what to do and not nearly enough time teaching them what not to do.' Urs does both beautifully with an engaging narrative."

—FRANK WAGNER, founding partner, Marshall Goldsmith Group, and cocreator of Stakeholder Centered Coaching®

"Urs Koenig has a rare résumé—champion ultraendurance athlete, MBA, PhD, military peacekeeper, and two decades as a top executive coach. From that set of unique experiences, he has crafted a powerful and (for many) counterintuitive statement on the nature of leadership and a necessary guide to the future of management thinking."

—JOSH LINKNER, five-time tech entrepreneur and *New York Times* best-selling author of *Disciplined Dreaming* and *Big Little Breakthroughs*

"*Radical Humility* gives us the vision and a step-by-step path to bring leadership into the NOW—a dynamic and rapidly changing world where old-school approaches often fall short. It's a must-read for anyone leading teams that span cultures and generations and can not only help corporate teams at any level but also leaders in politics, education, the military, and nonprofits. A fantastic contribution to next-generation leadership!"

—JENNIFER DUNCAN, former Africa Program director, senior attorney, and global policy advisor, Landesa

"In a world of increasing complexity and relentlessly shifting landscapes, the old-school, top-down way of leadership is obsolete. Humble leadership is the way of the future, and Urs Koenig has written the foundational guide."

—TIM CARVER, CEO, GQG Partners

"Now more than ever we need to develop, support, and champion leaders with the humanity to be 'tough on results, tender on people' and to unite teams at risk of being overwhelmed in an increasingly chaotic and polarized world. Urs Koenig's game-changing book is a motivational and inspirational guide to leading and living that—like its author—is authentic, tested in the toughest of conditions, and always leaves you with renewed purpose for the journey ahead."

—DAVID NELSON, entrepreneur, technology consultant, and former CEO

"As the world evolves, so too must our skills and abilities as leaders. *Radical Humility* reveals the mindset change that is needed to excel in the future. Just as Urs is as a person, his unique insights are approachable, engaging, and actionable. This book is an instructive and entertaining journey toward effective and meaningful leadership."

—LISA BRIDGE, president and CEO, Ben Bridge Jeweler, and president of the American Gem Society

"Having personally experienced the coaching and guidance of Urs Koenig, I can attest to the profound impact of the *Radical Humility* framework shared in this remarkable book. Urs's insights, conveyed through captivating stories, have revolutionized my own leadership approach, and now, through *Radical Humility*, he invites readers to embark on their own transformative journeys. This book offers a powerful blueprint for leaders seeking to navigate the complexities of our world with humility, authenticity, and success. Prepare to be inspired and transformed."

—VIC WALIA, CEO, BetCity

"*Radical Humility* presents a groundbreaking path to better leadership in our new world of work. By embracing humility as a core strength, Urs invites leaders to reconsider old paradigms and shed outdated approaches no longer serving us. With practical tools and profound insights, *Radical Humility* empowers leaders to cut through the noise, focus on what truly matters, and create more meaningful impact."

—SETH MATTISON, CEO, FutureSight Labs; cofounder, Impact Eleven; and author of *The Future of Leadership*

"In this uncertain world, we desperately need more badass leaders. We also need more outstandingly good humans. Urs guides us in how to bring out both of those qualities to be our best leader. Urs synthesizes hard-won lessons from the world of business, peacekeeping military service, and ultraendurance athletics to distill action-oriented lessons you can apply right now. Once I started reading *Radical Humility*, I could not put it down."

—PETER POLSON, CEO and founder, Tiller Money

"*Radical Humility* provides a comprehensive guide that delves into the essence of the type of leadership required for today's evolving workforce and world. The book provides valuable insights into individual growth, team dynamics, and organizational success. Urs provides real-world examples, research-backed insights, and practical strategies that are an answer to the call for a different type of leadership. This book equips leaders at all levels with the necessary understanding and tools (where many books stop short) to embrace humility in their leadership and day-to-day interactions. A must-read for leaders in health care who desire to serve with compassion and humility."

—TIFFANY NIEMAN, director of organizational development, OSF HealthCare

"From Pizza Hut to 7-Eleven to Centerplate, I've worked with some of the top management talent in the world. The 'secret sauce' for their success is exactly what Urs Koenig describes—a combination of confidence and humility that is (as Urs puts it) Tough on Results, Tender on People. This book should be required reading, whether you're leading one person or one hundred."

—DES HAGUE, eight-time CEO and author of *Fifteen Minutes of Shame*

"I served with Captain Urs Koenig in 2021 in my role as acting Head of Military, United Nations Truce Supervision Organization in the Middle East. Urs was one of my Military Experts on Mission during periods of heightened tension in the Levant. He is a tremendous military peacekeeper and representative of the Swiss Armed Forces. *Radical Humility* is an accessible and earthly account of leadership lessons, observations, and experiences—of equal utility and application to those serving in the profession of arms or those embarking on a business management or leadership pathway. His well-researched insights are grounded in theory as well as experience and delivered in an eminently readable and entertaining style. Read this book! You—and those you interact with—will be better for having done so. Results: they're achieved through people!"

—COLONEL MICHAEL SCOTT, CSC, Australian Army

"A culture of leadership where people do not feel safe to speak up lays the foundation for bad outcomes notwithstanding any short-term gains. *Radical Humility* helps create a much-needed alternative with a call to action to every leader to be your best self through self-awareness, compassion, understanding, openness, and connection. Urs is a master storyteller and brings a delightful combination of authenticity, practicality, and humaneness to leadership through a rich and varied set of experiences. A must-read for all leaders who dare to challenge themselves to do better and be better."

—THROSHNI NAIDOO, head of data platforms, Westpac Banking Corporation (Australia)

"In fifteen years in NFL and NBA boardrooms, I had a front-row seat to what separates elite performers from the rest of the pack—it's those who are tough on results and tender on people. This is how we build championship cultures that win and last. *Radical Humility* is a master class for it all."

—PAUL EPSTEIN, former NFL and NBA executive and bestselling author of *The Power of Playing Offense* and *Better Decisions Faster*

"Urs's storytelling and real-world examples of how humility can impact leadership are both insightful and relatable. From boardrooms to ultra-racing, Urs shows you how humbly connecting to people can create profound results. This book will help to unlock your leadership potential to become a more effective, empathetic, and successful leader."

—CHRIS RAGSDALE, ultraendurance champion

"Studies show that the majority of young adults believe that society is suffering from a crisis of leadership, with Gen Zers prioritizing empathy and honesty as two of the top traits they look for in a great leader. If you're looking to connect with the rising-star talent and get the most out of them, the unforgettable stories, actionable insights, and deeply researched framework in *Radical Humility* can help you become the boss everyone wants to work for."

—SANTOR NISHIZAKI, leadership expert and coauthor of *Working with Gen Z*

"Urs Koenig has synthesized monthslong executive coaching and leadership development programs into a timely and actionable book for today's leaders. If you are a no-nonsense hard driver, *Radical Humility* will provide you with the tools you need to still be a badass leader while also being a good human—in and out of the office."

—**CHARLIE LOZNER,** partner and vice president of digital media, Backbone Media

"*Radical Humility* is perfect for anyone trying to build, lead, and inspire teams to do the best work of their lives. If you're looking to take your leadership to the next level, read this book."

—**JEREMY BURGER,** CEO, Merriman Wealth Management

"Humility matters—now more than ever—and is central to tapping into the Ownership Mindset and taking control of your life and career. The Five Shifts outlined in *Radical Humility* are a cheat sheet to better knowing yourself, deepening and strengthening your relationships, and building the kind of culture of trust that increases productivity and makes people want to do their best work."

—**KERRY SIGGINS,** CEO, StoneAge, and author of *The Ownership Mindset*

"Being a loving and compassionate servant leader isn't about 'hugs and kisses'—it's about making sure your team members feel heard and valued. If they feel valued, they'll not only add value to the short-term bottom line but will contribute to a culture of growth and positivity for years to come. Urs Koenig understands this important truth, and *Radical Humility* is a road map for implementing this powerful type of leadership in your organization."

—**DAVID ZECHMAN,** author of *Driven by Compassion*

"This book has been an indispensable resource for me as a first-time CEO. The practical wisdom and actionable insights have been a guiding light, revolutionizing my approach to leadership. The *Radical Humility* framework has empowered me to lead with authenticity, fostering an organizational culture that values openness, empathy, and continuous growth. I am grateful for the transformation this book has brought not only to my professional life but also to my personal journey as a leader. This is not just a book—it's a life-changing experience for any leader embarking on their journey in this complex and ever-evolving world."

—MEHRDAD AFRAHI, CEO, 42 Inc.

# RADICAL HUMILITY

**www.amplifypublishinggroup.com**

*Radical Humility: Be a Badass Leader and a Good Human*

**For more information, please contact:**

Amplify Publishing, an imprint of Amplify Publishing Group
620 Herndon Parkway, Suite 220
Herndon, VA 20170
info@amplifypublishing.com

Library of Congress Control Number: 2023913546
CPSIA Code: PRV1023A
ISBN-13: 978-1-63755-405-0
Printed in the United States

*For my sons, Luc and Liam:*
*may you become the leaders our world needs*
*by embracing Radical Humility.*

*For my father, one of the best humble leaders*
*I have ever known: Papi, this is for you.*

# RADICAL HUMILITY

## BE A BADASS AND A GOOD
## LEADER HUMAN

# URS KOENIG

amplify
an imprint of Amplify Publishing Group

# CONTENTS

Introduction: That Damn Flak Jacket                                          1

Chapter 1: "With You, Captain—Anytime Again"                                 9

Chapter 2: The Time Is NOW for Humble Leadership                            23

## SHIFT I
## DIG DEEP                                                                  43

Chapter 3: Know Thyself                                                      45

Chapter 4: Focus Like an Elite Athlete                                      61

Chapter 5: Fail Successfully                                                77

## SHIFT II
## TOUGH ON RESULTS, TENDER ON PEOPLE                                        97

Chapter 6: Give a Damn about Others                                         101

Chapter 7: I Love You, and Your Work Is Not Good Enough                     117

## SHIFT III
## LEAD LIKE A COMPASS                                                      135

Chapter 8: Clarity over Control                                             137

Chapter 9: Build a Leadership Factory                                       149

## SHIFT IV
# FULL TRANSPARENCY                                    167

    Chapter 10: Here Is Where I Suck                   169

    Chapter 11: Share the Truth                       183


## SHIFT V
# CHAMPION A FEARLESS CULTURE                          203

    Chapter 12: Have Your People Rock the Boat        205

    Radical Humility . . . Close to Home               215

    Chapter 13: Build Fearless Teams                   221


    Your Call to Action                                247


    Acknowledgments                                    251

    Endnotes                                           255

    About the Author                                   269

# INTRODUCTION
## THAT DAMN FLAK JACKET

*The greatest enemy of learning is knowing.*
**—John Maxwell**

## Why Do We Need to Ask Better Questions?

It's 0700 on a dark, bitter cold January morning in the heart of Switzerland. The snow is blowing sideways. Despite all the layers I am wearing, I am cold deep into my bones. As I walk briskly toward my new comrades, I pull down my wool hat and bury my hands deep in my pockets. "Damn, it's freezing," I think. "What the hell have I done?"

Two days ago, I started my training to become a military peacekeeping commander. My comrades and I are now standing in a half circle facing a young sergeant who greets us with a booming, way-too-energetic "Guten Morgen!" Just as we respond with a collective, obligatory "Guten Morgen," the flak jacket (bulletproof vest) I am holding in my freezing hands slips through my fingers and collides with the frozen asphalt. *BOOM!*

The sergeant, twenty-five years my junior and well below my rank, slowly walks toward me, opens his mouth, and starts chewing me out like I am a naughty little schoolboy. But I am not. I'm almost fifty years old, and I've signed up for nine months of military peacekeeping service. Just a few days ago, I said a painful goodbye to my two young boys in Seattle. I left my family, my home, my friends, and a successful business to make a difference and be of service—and here I am being yelled at by some young punk.

It takes all the patience I have to not make a snarky comment. I swallow my pride and pick up my flak jacket . . . and say nothing at all. I do ask myself, though: "How can I make sure I never drop this damn vest ever again?"

Little do I know that having the self-awareness to stay silent instead of expressing my angry emotions in the moment will be one of many lessons in humility I'll learn during the next nine months.

■ ■ ■

Like every other Swiss male, I served in the military in my twenties. I'd been out of the service for almost twenty-two years when I decided to rejoin and serve in the international peacekeeping operation Kosovo Force (KFOR) in the Balkans. A main reason I joined the peacekeeping force was to make my own small contribution toward a more peaceful world. I also have a keen interest in conflict zones.

When we first deployed, I was overly confident. I was certain that I already understood the main dynamics of the conflict and the complex ethnic, socioeconomic, and political realities in Kosovo.

How wrong I was.

Four weeks into the deployment, my team and I were invited to an end-of-school-year celebration in one of the most remote villages in our area of responsibility (AOR). Representing KFOR, we were escorted to the front of the room, where we sat down and were treated to a forty-five-minute school play that was a reenactment of the deadly conflict more than two decades prior in the former Yugoslavia.

The play's main theme was the birth of the nation of Kosovo out of the ashes of the war. I watched in shock as eight- and nine-year-old kids reenacted hand-to-hand combat, shooting, and massacring their fellow students who were dressed as Serbs. All this to the roaring applause of parents, teachers, and politicians.

I arrived here thinking I *got* this conflict, yet sitting there, politely applauding, I realized how little I really knew. For the first time, I truly understood—in my heart, not just intellectually—that the contributions of my team and me, and indeed KFOR as a whole, while meaningful, were merely tiny pieces in what is an incredibly long, complicated journey toward peace and true reconciliation. It would take generations for Kosovo to get there.

Watching these first and second graders glorify the horrors of warfare, I felt disgust, anger, and a lot of judgment. But most of all, I felt incredibly humbled.

### Background: The Kosovo War, Kosovo Force (KFOR), and Swiss Peacekeepers

The Kosovo War lasted from February 28, 1998, to June 11, 1999. It was fought by the forces of the former Yugoslavia (i.e., Serbia and Montenegro), which controlled Kosovo before the war, and the Kosovo Albanian rebel group known as the Kosovo Liberation Army (KLA). NATO intervened with airstrikes in March 1999, which resulted in Yugoslav forces withdrawing. On the last day of the war, the NATO-led international peacekeeping unit known as Kosovo Force (KFOR) took command under a UN Security Council resolution. At that time, Kosovo faced a grave humanitarian crisis with nearly one million displaced people and numerous mass killings of civilians.

KFOR's mission, which continues to this day, is building a secure environment and guaranteeing the freedom of movement throughout Kosovo for all citizens, regardless of their ethnic origin. Switzerland has a sizeable diaspora from Kosovo, so my home country has a direct interest in the region's stability. This is the main reason the Swiss Armed Forces have participated in KFOR since 1999 with a contingent of around 200 troops. Even though armed conflicts are contained in Kosovo thanks to the presence of KFOR, ethnic tension between Albanians and Serbs remains high to this day and leads to occasional violence.[1]

On the drive back to our team's base, I asked myself: How can we shape and influence the stories children in Kosovo get taught at home and in school so true reconciliation between future generations of Serbs and Albanians becomes possible? Is it our place as peacekeepers to try to build peace in people's hearts as well as in their cities?

It dawned on me that even though I might never have the answers, I must continue to ask questions that are not about me. Within a few months from dropping my flak jacket, my questions shifted from a self-centered "How can I ensure I never, ever drop this damn thing ever again?" to "How might we need to reimagine our role as peacekeepers to move this young nation to lasting peace?"

Asking questions about topics bigger than ourselves is one element of Radical Humility, which, as you will see, is a new kind of leadership our world needs now.

## My Evolving Interest in Humility

I'd been intrigued by the concept of humility throughout my career, well before I was deployed to Kosovo. As a competitive ultraendurance athlete, businessman, executive coach, and professor, I was drawn to leaders who let their accomplishments speak for themselves and who shone the light on their teams, not themselves.

I was also inspired by people who, despite successes, never stopped learning and growing. For example, in the notoriously macho ultracycling racing scene, I got along best with fellow competitors who let their legs do the talking rather than their big mouths. The same was true in my many other athletic, academic, and business endeavors—I loved hanging around humble achievers. But I did not study their traits with any seriousness.

In the aftermath of the financial crisis in 2007–08, as technology started to evolve at an ever-faster pace and social media use exploded, something started to shift with my executive coaching clients that got me to examine humility with more rigor. I observed many of my clients becoming overwhelmed with the growing speed, complexity, and messiness of the business environment in which they led their teams. My clients seemed to always be a step behind, and as their coach, it pained me to watch them struggle. Experiencing their battles drove me to ask myself: How do we best lead in this new world that is uniquely complex, fast moving, chaotic, and deeply interconnected?

Seeking answers to this question got me digging into the role that humility plays in leadership. Not that I needed much convincing, but my studies sold me on humility as a desirable *personal trait* for a leader. But I was less sure about how humility in leadership could have wider-ranging organizational benefits, let alone be the answer to leading successfully in a complex world.

My view of humility further evolved when I rejoined the military as a peace-keeper in 2017. Ironically, transitioning back into a traditional, hierarchical organization provided countless opportunities to experience firsthand how humility is essential to leading successfully. The very personal and impactful learnings around humility during my deployment in Kosovo inspired me to embark on a journey to systematically research how humility helps us lead in today's world.

This book is the result of that quest.

*Radical Humility: Be a Badass Leader and a Good Human* is full of insights and takeaways I have gained during that time and throughout my thirty-five years in leadership positions in business, academia, ultraendurance sports, and the military while living and working on four continents. While my research is backed by a solid body of academic work, I won't bombard you with high-flying academic theories or BS consulting jargon.

## Who Should Read This Book?

This book has been written from the trenches of leadership. It is intended to make a difference in the real world for anyone tasked with delivering results every day with their teams, whether you're a manager, business owner, director, VP, or C-level executive.

But it is not only for people in executive roles with official titles. Leadership is more than a position. Leadership is a set of cooperative relationships that maximizes the efforts of others to achieve something bigger and better. Or more simply, leadership is getting important stuff done through and with other people. As such, this book is not only for people in formal leadership roles but for anyone working in an environment where they need more than just their individual actions to achieve the desired results. So team members can benefit from this book too.

Really, this book is vital for anybody who desires and needs to lead teams to high performance under their watch in an increasingly tumultuous world ... anybody who wants to experience the benefits of designing and leading teams that are based on more open, trusting, and cooperative relationships.

## Radical Humility

The book's overarching thesis is that achieving strong results in today's world requires a new kind of leadership that embraces three tenets: self-knowledge, a focus on strong relationships, and a growth mindset. These are the core aspects of Radical Humility.

I chose *Radical* as the concept for this book because I want to emphasize that you cannot half-ass humility. I will capitalize the term throughout the book. However, to make the text more readable, I will sometimes shorten Radical Humility to simply *humility*.

Humility often gets a bad rap because it's associated with weakness. People resist it because they think being humble means they lack confidence and ambition or that they can't assert themselves. But that's not true. You can be humble *and* ambitious. You can be humble *and* assertive. You can be humble *and* tough, demanding, and confident.

The chapters that follow show specifically what Radical Humility is, why it works, and most notably, how to achieve it.

## THEN to NOW: The Journey to Radical Humility

My experiences and research led me to identify what I call the Five THEN to NOW Shifts that help us to lead with Radical Humility.

THEN Leadership is what leaders relied on in the past. THEN Leadership is heavy-handed, top-down, command-and-control. It is so-called heroic or expert leadership—concepts that are too simplistic and too fraught with worshipping centralized, authoritarian tendencies that lead to counterproductive and even dangerous results.

In contrast, NOW Leadership is about knowing and growing ourselves and our colleagues. It is about asking questions. Sharing and distributing power. Being honest and being transparent. Forming trusting relationships. Valuing people as whole individuals. NOW Leadership is also about holding ourselves and others accountable.

Put simply, leading with Radical Humility = NOW Leadership.

Here are the Five Shifts that take us from THEN to NOW:

## SHIFT I: DIG DEEP

*From Blind Spots (THEN) to Self-Awareness (NOW)*

## SHIFT II: TOUGH ON RESULTS, TENDER ON PEOPLE

*From Heavy-Handed (THEN) to High-Touch, High Standards (NOW)*

## SHIFT III: LEAD LIKE A COMPASS

*From Micromanaging (THEN) to Empowerment (NOW)*

## SHIFT IV: FULL TRANSPARENCY

*From Secrecy and Avoidance (THEN) to Transparency and Openness (NOW)*

## SHIFT V: CHAMPION A FEARLESS CULTURE

*From Afraid to Speak Up (THEN) to Fearless Culture (NOW)*

The Five Shifts are organized in a logical progression from leading self (Shift I) to leading teams (Shifts II, III, and IV) to leading organizations (Shift V).

You can easily jump back and forth between chapters as your world demands it and as you want a quick review or dose of inspiration or support. Each chapter is filled with case studies, stories, and personal anecdotes— many from my leadership in military peacekeeping and other professional domains—as well as principles, practices, and engaging exercises.

While I am confident this book will provide you with many new insights, I *really* hope that you will act on the learnings in this book for yourself and your teams.

Throughout the book you will find "NOW Leadership . . . NOW" prompts that you can implement immediately. These are designed to help you elevate your leadership by applying Radical Humility to everyday situations you face.

You will also find further resources, tool kits, and exercises by scanning the QR codes provided to ensure the learning continues well beyond this book. I would love to hear what you are learning from these applications. Drop me a note at **urs@urskoenig.com**.

No matter where you are on your leadership journey, my desire is to help transform you into a humble leader who builds amazing teams that achieve stellar results.

Become a badass leader and a good human, and join me in the Radical Humility movement.

Let's dive in . . .

# CHAPTER 1
# "WITH YOU, CAPTAIN—ANYTIME AGAIN"

*It is well to remember that the entire universe,*
*with one trifle exception, is composed of others.*
**—John Holmes, American poet (1904–1962)**

## What Is Humble Leadership?

On the first day of reporting to my military peacekeeping command duties, I realized I did not even know how to dress myself. I was almost fifty years old, and I did not know how to put my military uniform on, let alone properly holster my handgun. Having been out of the service for twenty-two years, I found that my military knowledge was outdated. My subordinates knew much more than I did, yet I was their commander.

To gain their respect and complete our mission successfully, I knew I needed to lead by relationship rather than expertise. I started to practice one of the cornerstones of Radical Humility. I started by building strong, collaborative relationships with my team as well as across and up and down the entire peacekeeping force. I invested heavily in social capital.

After three months of intense peacekeeping training, during which we really got to know one another well, my team and I deployed to Kosovo at the end of March 2017. But we were short two key team members. My deputy commander and our warrant officer, the person responsible for all our logistics and the base's infrastructure, were assigned to us at the last minute just after we deployed. My number two in charge was important for me to have on board.

The warrant officer was just as critical. We were stationed as a totally independent unit in a team base many miles away from the closest military camp. For all intents and purposes, we were on our own, and the warrant officer was responsible for everything from making sure we had enough ammunition and food to ensuring the base was kept clean and that we had heat, electricity, and running water.

I arrived in Kosovo having never met two of my mission-critical team members, and I needed to establish trust, engagement, and open communication quickly.

The first thing I did was take them to lunch and learn as much as I could about them personally: their families, professional experiences, hobbies, passions, and plans after the mission. I also inquired about their hopes and fears about our upcoming mission together and their expectations of me as their commander.

Among other things I learned that my deputy commander was a recovering Swiss banker, an adrenaline junkie who enjoyed skydiving and paragliding, and that she was unsure about her next professional move after the mission. I learned that my warrant officer was a trained chef who despite his young age had worked extensively in high-end kitchens around the globe. He was saving money for his studies in hotel management after the mission and was very close to his family.

It helps that I love people, but these one-on-ones also had a clear purpose. Building collaborative relationships and trust, I knew, would make it easier for us to rely on one another when the famous stuff hit the fan—as it inevitably would.

I followed these initial lunch meetings up with regular one-on-one meetings with each member of the team for the duration of the whole mission, during which I continued to inquire about their professional and personal well-being as well as invite feedback on my performance as their leader. I cared about them and valued their opinions.

Because I showed genuine interest in each of them as a whole person and not just the roles they were fulfilling for me, we bonded right away. This in turn enabled me to delegate and empower quickly.

For example, I tasked my deputy commander very early on in the deployment with the responsibility for an inspection of our team base by high-level members of the peacekeeping force because I was absent on short notice. As part of the inspection, she had to give several briefings to numerous high-ranking officers. My deputy was understandably very nervous, but thanks to our collaborative relationship founded on trust and transparency, she was prepared to take on this crucial task and pulled it off brilliantly.

My leadership during the peacekeeping mission was by no means perfect, and of course I made plenty of mistakes. However, leading by relationships helped my team to achieve one of the highest performance ratings of all the teams in the peacekeeping force, and we fulfilled the mission to the fullest satisfaction of our commanders. Leading relationally also earned me the biggest compliment I could ever wish for.

At the end of our nine months together, several of my team members made a point of looking me in the eye and saying, "With you, Captain—anytime again." That is something I am very proud of, and I attribute it in large part to the strong relationships we built in our team—which, as you will see, is one of the cornerstones of leading with Radical Humility.

And just to be clear, the irony of me bragging a bit about my own humility is not lost on me. Yet as we will discover throughout this book, leading with Radical Humility does not mean we can't talk about our achievements. You can be assertive, highly driven, and ambitious and still join us.

## Defining Humble Leadership

I have so far shared the importance of a growth mindset by asking big questions and leading relationally. There is another crucial element of Humble Leadership, and that is better self-knowledge. Based on the existing humble leadership literature from academics and practitioners[1] and my own research, I define humble leadership along the following dimensions:

1. **Self-Knowledge:** Developing true self-awareness. Radical Humility means having an *accurate* understanding of yourself, both embracing your strengths and talents while owning your shortcomings and weaknesses. Humility does not mean having low self-esteem or never talking about your strengths. Much like self-centered narcissism that overvalues your strengths, having an overtly low opinion of yourself is not humble. And both lack accuracy.

2. **Leading Relationally—Team:** Seeing yourself as part of a two-way relationship with others you manage, report to, and work with. Leading with Radical Humility means building trusting and cooperative relationships with those around you and communicating to them that you value them as whole people and not just as human resources who get tasks done for you.

3. **Leading Relationally—Organization:** Seeing yourself in relation to the larger whole. You see yourself as *one* actor in the play versus *the* main character. You realize that in today's complex world, no one person can have all the answers and do it all. Humble organizational leadership requires you to understand and actively develop the interpersonal and group dynamics of many people and take full responsibility for driving how team members interact. Humble leaders know how to transform teams into high-performing units where everybody feels safe to speak up and contribute and in the process champion a fearless team culture.

4. **Growth Mindset:** Embracing constant learning and growing. It is reframing failure as an important growth opportunity versus something to be ashamed of, or even worse, to cover up. Instead of protecting the perfect hero leader façade, a growth mindset embraces failure as a key component of innovation and growth, then modeling this for your teams (I will discuss the growth mindset in more depth in chapter 3).

Applying a growth mindset is foundational to the first three dimensions of Humble Leadership (1. Self-Knowledge, 2. Leading Relationally—Team, and 3. Leading Relationally—Organization). This is demonstrated in the Humble Leadership Framework (figure 1.1), which is the skeleton on which we will add the five NOW Leadership shifts I will introduce in chapter 2. That will serve as our guide for the course of this book.

*Figure 1.1: The Humble Leadership Framework*

**Self-Knowledge/ Growth Mindset**

**Leading Relationally (Team)/ Growth Mindset**

**Leading Relationally (Org.)/ Growth Mindset**

**HUMBLE LEADERSHIP = NOW LEADERSHIP**

I often get asked how humble leadership differs from other leadership models such as servant and transformational leadership. Because humble leadership emphasizes the development of cooperative and trusting personal relationships, it serves as the foundation for these models. You can't serve your people as a *servant leader* if you have not gotten to know them on a meaningful personal level. To effectively lead and mentor them, you need to understand their unique strengths and challenges.

The same applies to *transformational leadership*. Only if you humbly park your ego at the door and let your team members shine will you inspire your people to go above and beyond their own self-interests for the advancement of your team and organization. That creates true transformation. So rather than it being a competing model, humble leadership supports and drives servant and transformational leadership.

## The Origins of Humble Leadership

The English word *humility* originates from the Latin *humus*, or "of the ground or earth," meaning close to the ground or earth. Many ancient philosophers viewed humility as desirable. They advocated that we keep our ego in check by purposefully lowering ourselves close to the ground.[2]

Humility is also a core value in all major world religions, including Buddhism, Christianity, Hinduism, Islam, and Judaism. All world religions remind us that we are members of a species that is far from perfect and urge us to be mindful of our limited role in the fate of the world.[3]

In the leadership arena, prior to the twenty-first century, humility was primarily seen as a trait defined by weakness. Then, in 2001, Jim Collins published the business bestseller *Good to Great: Why Some Companies Make the Leap and Others Don't.*[4] It was the first evidence-based research on leadership and humility, and it made the compelling case that humble leaders are the most successful ones.

Even though *Good to Great* was published more than twenty years ago and some of the companies that Collins classified as great back then have been less so over the years (Wells Fargo and Fannie Mae come to mind), it remains an important piece of work on humble leadership. Collins found that the strongest leaders are not the headline-making, larger-than-life personalities who end up as celebrities. Instead, he discovered great leaders are those who blend personal humility with iron personal will. Collins calls this Level 5 leadership: when there is success, Level 5 leaders look out the window; when there is failure, they look in the mirror.

The early twenty-first century has seen a string of business leadership scandals. Enron (2001), Freddie Mac (2003), Lehman Brothers (2008), Bernie Madoff (2008), BP (2010), Volkswagen (VW) (2015), Wells Fargo (2016), Uber (2017), Boeing (2018), and FTX (2022), among others, forced fundamental questions about what kind of leadership we are teaching in business school and what kind of leadership we need today. Perhaps that is why humility started appearing in the business press and academic leadership literature around 2010.[5]

Simultaneously, a small number of leadership books on the importance of humility were published. Most notable is the terrific book *Humble Leadership:*

*The Power of Relationships, Openness, and Trust* by one of the fathers of the field of organizational development, former MIT professor Edgar Schein, coauthored with Silicon Valley consultant Peter Schein.[6] *Humble Leadership* postulates a new kind of leadership based on trusting personal relationships to make possible collaborative problem-solving and innovation.

The COVID-19 pandemic did its part to bring humility front and center to the leadership conversation. When the world shut down, we all had to acknowledge how little control we really have over the course of the world and our own lives. Leaders at all levels had to humbly admit they did not know what the future might bring. We all had to adapt as we went.

Research on business practices during this pivotal era is still being developed, but if you're like me, you've seen many examples since 2020 in leadership literature, the business press, and general news articles where leaders have acknowledged how essential humility was to getting through traumatic times. I've seen it with my clients and friends—humility didn't just allow people and organizations to survive the pandemic; in many cases, it helped them thrive during and after it. Perhaps that was true for you too.

Two caveats up front:

1. It would be presumptuous (and clearly not humble) of me to claim that leading with Radical Humility provides all the answers on how to succeed. The world is too complex for that. Leadership experts and countless leaders within organizations are focused and highly motivated to determine how to best lead in our messy and uber-networked world. So with humility I will state that leadership is difficult in the best of times, and there are many paths to success. The situational leadership approach[7] has long argued that different situations and contexts require different leadership styles. For example, a crisis might mean a command-and-control leadership approach is temporarily most appropriate. When the house is on fire, that's no time for relationship building.

   Not to get ahead of myself, but while top-down, command-and-control might be called for in an acute crisis and may look deceptively appealing to implement more aggressively and permanently, the main argument of this book is that humble leadership is the key to success in highly complex and fast-moving environments. But the bricks must be laid and the foundation must be built before the stuff hits the fan!

2. Humility is no replacement for competence and skill. As humble leaders, we must constantly strive to learn about ourselves and our team members as well as how to build a strong culture. We also must keep improving our technical competencies. If we don't, we lose all credibility. This is an absolute nonnegotiable.

   In my opening story, I shared how I had a military knowledge gap when I first reported to my peacekeeping command. I was keenly aware of it. I was open and transparent with my team and asked them for support when I needed it, but at the same time, I worked my butt off studying, asking lots of questions, and soaking up as much as I could so that my technical skills were up to par within weeks of starting training.

Having gotten these two caveats out of the way, let's together dismantle three common myths and then discover two surprising and fun truths about humility and leadership.

## Three Myths and Two Surprising Truths about Humility and Leadership

Humility often gets a bad rap because it is associated with weakness. But humble leaders are, in fact, fundamentally confident, decisive, and ambitious.

### Myth #1: Leaders Cannot Be Both Humble and Confident

Not only is this false, but I believe you *must* be confident to lead with humility in order to share credit.

This connection between confidence and humility might seem counter-intuitive at first, but think about it: Vulnerability is required to share your own weaknesses and where you need to improve. However, only if you are confident in yourself are you able to handle the implications of your humility—really hear the feedback and act on it. I know it is much harder for me to invite feedback when I am already a bit down on myself. To humbly invite others to honestly tell me what they think of my leadership, I need to have confidence that despite all my weaknesses, I have many strengths and that I am fundamentally OK and can effectively deal with the feedback provided.

Further, only if you feel comfortable in your own skin can you empower, delegate comprehensively, and enable frontline decision-making. As a humble leader, you are confident in your ability to create, train, and develop an expert team—step out of the spotlight and let them do the jobs they were hired and trained for. Rather than being a contradiction, confidence and humility go hand in hand.

### Myth #2: Leaders Cannot Be Both Humble and Decisive

Conventional wisdom might suggest that humble leaders are indecisive—afraid to act when the negotiation is on the line or a team needs direction in crisis. Jim Collins's research in *Good to Great* showed the opposite, that Level 5 leaders are those who blend personal humility with iron personal will to make tough calls. They blend humility and decisiveness to take charge and change direction when needed, all in the service of bettering the organization and producing long-term results.

### Myth #3: Leaders Cannot Be Both Humble and Ambitious

It requires self-assurance to question your assumptions and reconsider what you always thought was true. *What business are we in? Why are we failing? What is my part in this?* These are hard, often painful, things to ask, yet they're necessary if you are serious about reaching massive goals.

Only by constantly learning and growing can you make necessary changes to truly succeed. And striving for success is indeed the very definition of ambition.

One of the more frequently quoted *Good to Great* leaders is Darwin Smith, former CEO of Kimberly-Clark. After his retirement, he reflected on his secret for success. In his humble words, "I never stopped trying to become qualified for the job."[8]

Oprah Winfrey is another powerful example of a highly ambitious and humble leader. She was born into poverty to a single teenage mother. Oprah became pregnant at fourteen; her son was born prematurely and died in infancy. She landed a job in radio while still in high school. By nineteen, she was a coanchor for the local evening news, and her astonishing entrepreneurial career took off from there.

Dubbed the Queen of All Media, she became the first female Black billionaire. She has been ranked as one of the most influential women in the world.[9] Though she has at times been criticized for having an overly emotion-centered approach, there is no doubt that Oprah has ambitiously overcome tremendous adversity. She has also benefited millions around the globe by helping make humility and self-awareness more mainstream, all while keeping her ego in check.

Smith and Oprah remind us that even when we are highly successful, we always have lots more to learn and master. Humility allows us to apply a growth mindset and always strive to do better.

### Surprising Truth #1: "I Am the Captain, but I Am Not Better Than Anyone Else"

Sam Walker, in his painstakingly thorough book *The Captain Class: A New Theory of Leadership*,[10] pulled off the *Good to Great* version for the world of team sports. Applying rigorous criteria, he identified the best teams across all team sports over the history of organized competition. Sounds daunting, right? Starting with thousands and thousands of teams, he narrowed it down to seventeen teams that dominated at the very top level for a long period of time competing against the best of the best. Among them are the New York

Yankees (1945–1953); the Pittsburgh Steelers (1974–1980); the New Zealand Rugby National Team, a.k.a. the All Blacks (2011–2018); the Cuban women's volleyball team (1991–2000); and the US women's soccer team (1996–1999).

He then asked this question: What, if anything, do these outstanding teams have in common? The answer is surprising: it's not loads of money, a large talent pool, or an amazing coaching staff. The dominance of *all* seventeen top-class teams corresponded with the arrival and departure of one particular player who was or would eventually become captain.

What's more, these seventeen captains lacked superstar talent, avoided the spotlight, and had other characteristics in common: they combined extreme doggedness, focus, and aggressive play with a humble willingness to do the thankless jobs in the shadows. They all had a low-key, practical, and democratic communication style.

Walker's research mirrors the findings of Collins's *Good to Great* Level 5 leadership (combine iron will with personal humility). The result? The best sports teams of all time are all led by humble leaders!

For example, the captain of the US women's soccer team, Carla Overbeck, scored only seven goals in her entire international career, which is low even for a defender. The very moment she had possession of the ball, she would look for ways to pass it—astonishingly, even when she had a chance to score herself. On and off the field, she displayed great humility and would often carry her teammates' bags to their hotel rooms after especially grueling international flights.

"I am the captain," she explained, "but I am not better than anyone else. I'm certainly not a better soccer player." In training, out of the eye of the public, Overbeck pushed herself and her teammates relentlessly. Her incredible work ethic and passing on the field and her humility and bag-schlepping off of it allowed her to amass massive capital with her teammates that she could spend when it was needed. She used it, for example, to be firm when holding them accountable for mistakes or to motivate them when they were not giving it their all during a conditioning drill.[11]

## Surprising Truth #2: Humility Makes You Smarter

What is the most important characteristic you want to teach your children to help them get high grades at school? Hard work? Thoroughness? Self-confidence? No doubt those are all important, but as it turns out, what is even more important for getting good grades is being humble.

In a remarkable study, Professor Bradley Owen, one of the foremost academic experts on humble leadership, surveyed and measured the performance of 144 students at the University of Washington in my hometown of Seattle.[12] Over the course of the management class, students took a mental ability test as well as several other psychological assessments and rated one another on humility.

The results showed the most important predictor of a student's overall performance was humility. It's more important than mental ability (a.k.a. smarts), self-efficacy, and conscientiousness. What's more, humility was the best predictor of how much a student improved between midterm and final exam. Humility even compensated for mental ability, meaning students who scored lower on that test were able to keep up with "smarter" kids if they were humbler. According to the research, the reasons for these surprising findings are as follows:

1. Humble students are more willing to ask for and receive feedback from their professors and fellow students. They are also more willing to act on it.
2. They more accurately assessed themselves, which made them better at realistically planning how much time and effort they needed to study for exams (we will cover the importance of knowing thyself in chapter 3).
3. Humble students were more likely to appreciate the habits of strong students and then successfully model their behavior accordingly, which increased their own performance.

A quick personal sidenote here: As a dad and even before I was aware of this study, I have been emphasizing the importance of humility, especially as it pertains to study habits, with my boys. I remember my younger son, Liam, working hard on a middle school geography project that the teacher did not initially seem impressed with. By embracing the humble skill of frequently checking in with his teacher and proactively asking for feedback on what specifically he could do better, as well as emulating some of the habits of the strongest students in his class, he was able to significantly improve his final project, earning him an excellent grade.

Want your kids to get high grades? Teach them to humbly ask for feedback, know themselves, and model the behavior of their strongest peers.

■ ■ ■

I have defined Humble Leadership; shown that confidence, decisiveness, and ambition go hand in hand with it; and explained why humility is crucial for success in sport and at school. In chapter 2, I will demonstrate why Humble Leadership is key to winning in our complex world . . . NOW.

## Assessing Your Radical Humility

First, though, it's your turn to assess where you stand when it comes to Radical Humility. Whether you have believed those myths in the past or found those truths particularly surprising, whether you are just starting out or are well on your way, having a baseline to draw from will help you determine what you need to work on to become a more effective leader.

Scan the QR code below to take the Radical Humility Assessment. You'll get a personalized score and a rundown of your Radical Humility gaps that will be useful as you go through this book and commit to Humble Leadership in your daily life.

# CHAPTER 2
# THE TIME IS NOW FOR HUMBLE LEADERSHIP

*When you are finished changing, you're finished.*
**—Benjamin Franklin**

## Why Is Humble Leadership the Key to Winning in Our Complex World?

On September 30, 2004, General Stanley McChrystal, head of the Joint Special Operations Command fighting terrorism in the Middle East, sat in his command center at Balad airbase in Iraq. He was surrounded by his team when he received news about the most devastating suicide attack yet in the war. Just sixty miles south of where he was sitting, two cars had sped into a huge crowd gathered for the opening ceremony for a new sewer plant. Thirty-five children lay dead; 10 Americans and 140 Iraqis were wounded.

As General Stanley McChrystal writes in his outstanding book *Team of Teams: New Rules of Engagement for a Complex World,*[1] he had come to this painful realization: Al Qaeda did not operate in Iraq like terrorist groups of the past had around the world. It was a decentralized network that could move quickly, strike ruthlessly, then vanish into the local population.

The allied forces had huge advantages in number of troops, training, and equipment, but none of that seemed to matter. But instead of giving stricter orders, taking more actions, or making bigger decisions, McChrystal instead first turned to his team and asked them questions: "If we are the best of the best, why are such deadly attacks increasing? Why are we unable to defeat an underresourced insurgency? Why are children dying? Why are our soldiers dying? Why?"

One thing was clear to McChrystal and his team: his task force was structured and led in a very traditional and hierarchical way—lots of silos. This centralized (THEN) decision-making structure made it too slow to adapt to a nimbler (NOW) enemy. This outdated leadership structure cost hundreds of lives and was on the verge of costing the allied forces the war on terror.

McChrystal had the humility to recognize he needed to change his leadership. He moved from a classic command-and-control approach, which he called leading like a chess master, to leading like a gardener. Yes, a gardener. As a gardener, you can't actually make plants grow—just like as a leader, you can't actually make your team do what you want. What you can and must do when leading like a gardener is plant the right seedlings at the right time in the right spot, nurture them, and provide them a healthy environment by watering and weeding so that your plants—your people—can thrive.

Over the months and years that followed, gardener McChrystal rebuilt the task force's culture around the systematic and purposeful development of trusting relationships, transparent sharing of information, and intentional culture building. By taking an interest in his people, McChrystal understood the core of humble leadership. As he put it, "'Thank you' became my most important phrase, interest and enthusiasm my most important behaviors."[2]

As a result of these leadership shifts, the task force became measurably more effective, its speed and precision improving by a factor of seventeen.[3]

McChrystal's THEN to NOW transformation is a powerful example of Radical Humility in action. He is one of the first prominent leaders to consciously embrace humble leadership. McChrystal was a tough military leader, yet he had the ability to recognize that he needed to change the way he led his task force. In his words, "Few of us are criticized if we faithfully do what has worked many times before. But feeling comfortable or dodging criticism should not be our measure of success. There is likely a place in paradise for people who tried hard, but what really matters is succeeding. If that requires you to change, that's your mission."[4] McChrystal is the living embodiment of the idea that humble leaders can also be ambitious, confident, and tough.

## The Fog of Work

Most people never face what McChrystal and his troops faced in the field against relentless networks of determined Al Qaeda fighters, but like Al Qaeda, our environment today is embedded with ever-changing variables constantly in play—increasing global interconnectivity, transformational technological advances, and an increasingly diverse workforce.

VUCA, a term first coined by the US Army War College, describes our current world well: Volatile, Uncertain, Complex, and Ambiguous. Situations evolve quickly with just-in-time transfer of information.

Bear with me for some brief historical background: Developed societies have moved from the Industrial Age to the Network Age, using the bridge of the Information Age (table 2.1). The Network Age is the business version of the "fog of war," the term used to refer to the great uncertainty experienced by commanders and soldiers overwhelmed by the messy, urgent realities on the battlefield. These days, all aspects of life and business can feel confusing and disheartening. It's the "fog of work."

*Table 2.1: Industrial Age to Network Age*

| Industrial Age (THEN) | Network Age (NOW) via Information Age |
| --- | --- |
| Silos | Networks |
| Complicated | Complex |
| Linear | Nonlinear |
| Slow connectivity | Just-in-time interconnectivity |
| Predicting | Configuring |
| Producing for "the Man" | Meaningful work |
| Individualism | Team-based work |

The Industrial Age was characterized by mechanical, linear, and predictable relationships (think the factory floor in the classic Charlie Chaplin movie *Modern Times*). It was complicated, but it was also linear and predictable, with clearly defined rules.

In the mid-twentieth century, we moved into the still-ongoing Information Age through the rapid development and rise of computer and chip technology. The availability of data and information exploded for anyone, anywhere with a keyboard and a click of a mouse. This exponential growth has only accelerated—tapping and swiping are that much quicker—and we have catapulted into the Network Age.

Our networked world is characterized by complexity: fast-moving, nonlinear relationships and ever-changing networks. Social media, for example, has enabled geographically dispersed social groups to mobilize within minutes. This has fundamentally shaken the foundation of traditional top-down leadership.

Overlaying these changes are generational dynamics. Generations Y and Z are redefining the meaning of work for themselves. More than just a source of income (THEN), a career needs to be fulfilling in its own right, have a purpose beyond a paycheck, and make a difference in the world (NOW). These emerging generations want to identify with the larger mission of organizations. And many of them can (and want to) work from anywhere, especially from home, a trend accelerated by the pandemic.

But it's not just age diversity. Our teams are becoming increasingly varied across many dimensions: ethnicity, gender, sexual orientation, political outlook, and many more. The US census data, for example, shows that people who identify as white and non-Hispanic (the current largest US racial population) declined in numbers for the first time on record in 2020 to 58 percent, down from 64 percent in 2010. By 2045, more than half of all Americans are projected to belong to what is now considered a minority group.[5] Diverse teams are a tremendous asset for any organization because of the wide-ranging perspectives represented, but leading them has unique challenges.[6]

To make things even more trying, organizations have become less local (THEN) and more global (NOW) in reach, and work is increasingly team based, even when the team is geographically dispersed. Today we spend 50 percent more time collaborating than we did twenty years ago.[7] Hiring great talent alone is not enough anymore. Your people must be able to work well together, and it is your job to create the right culture to make this happen.[8]

What does this mean for you as a leader? We used to have weeks and months (THEN) to analyze a situation, develop a plan of action, communicate that plan, and then execute it. Today's world (NOW) demands that far-reaching decisions be made on the spot by your team, independently, and because of the time pressure, with little guidance from leadership. Oh, and your team members might be eight time zones removed from you, twenty years younger (or older!) than you, speak a different native language, and live and work in a different culture.

How has our leadership evolved in response to the demands of this new world? Not very well.

## Heroic Leadership: An Outdated THEN Concept

Much of our leadership philosophy to this day is still deeply rooted in the Industrial Age mindset, when leadership was strictly role and rule based and the man in charge—and it was almost always a man—sat on top of the org chart and controlled all movement from there. Simplistically, the leader was often portrayed in the organization and media as the sole know-it-all expert who had all the answers. He was a "hero" who was impeccable. Interactions with subordinates were hierarchical, strictly role based, and transactional in nature, where what you could do for the boss and organization was all the leader cared about.

Our response in this new world, unfortunately, has been in many ways to work harder and faster but in the same old-school fashion. Instead of pausing and asking ourselves what kind of new leadership is required, we are attempting to fine-tune the same old, outdated models. In short, we have focused on becoming more efficient (doing things right) versus becoming more effective (doing the right things).

While the world is becoming more VUCA (Volatile, Uncertain, Complex, and Ambiguous), we are still designing our organizations and teams in the linear, predictable, mechanical way (figure 2.1).

Figure 2.1: The VUCA (Volatile, Uncertain, Complex, and Ambiguous) World vs. Typical Organizations[9]

**The VUCA World**   *vs.*   **Typical Organizations**

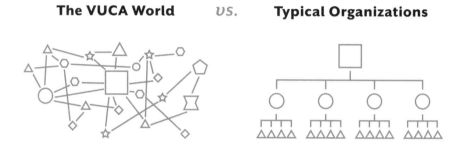

Given the increased speed and complexity of information, old-school leaders are often overwhelmed and cannot keep up. As sole decision-makers at the top, they become the bottleneck. By the time the decision leaves the leader's desk, it's too late to have a meaningful impact. Whatever that decision was, it's now at least an iteration behind. The self-centered, heroic "look what I have done" leadership that is so deeply ingrained in folks climbing the corporate ladder is out and does not deliver the results we need in today's world.

Figure 2.2 shows different leadership styles as a function of the kind of relationship you have with your people (from transactional to collaborative) and across time (from Industrial Age to Network Age).

- In the bottom left sits heroic leadership that worked well in the Industrial Age, when things were predictable and linear and the main focus of leadership was efficiency. Relationships with team members were transactional, and team members were seen as easily replaceable cogs in a wheel.

- The top left quadrant is what I call paternalistic leadership. These were the rare leaders during the Industrial Age who built collaborative relationships with their people.
- The bottom right quadrant is where the breakdown occurs and where many leaders are still stuck today. The Network Age requires collaborative relationships that empower, build up, and allow for constant learning and growing—yet we remain on a transactional relationship level.
- Finally, the top right is Radically Humble Leadership, and of course, it's where we want to be—tackling the Network Age with deeper, more meaningful personal and collaborative relationships with our team members.

*Figure 2.2: Different Leadership Styles as a Function of Strength of Relationship and across Time*

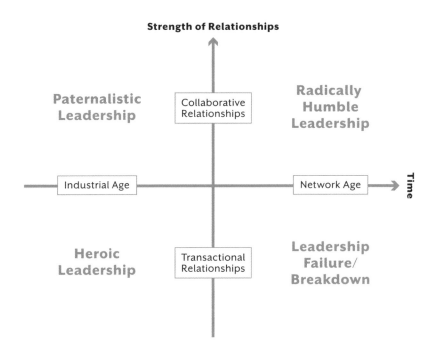

## The VUCA World Requires Humble Leadership

As leaders in the Network Age, you are facing what McChrystal calls an *inversion of expertise*,[10] meaning your people know so much more than you do about their specific area, yet you are their leader. Leaders are by definition generalists. In our tumultuous world, it is impossible for one individual to accumulate enough knowledge to figure it all out.

Successfully leading in the Network Age is therefore humbling. We need to acknowledge that complexity, ambiguity, and an ever-shifting competitive landscape are here to stay. You must display the humility to recognize you cannot figure it all out yourself and that you need a strong and empowered team to help you do so.

Instead of heavy-handed, centralized leadership from the top, our world requires you to relentlessly communicate and model a shared purpose across your teams so that you can empower front-line execution. It requires you to build resilient, highly adaptable teams. This involves breaking down silos and working across departments to master flexible responses. It involves individuals and teams sharing with full transparency with others what they know and also what they struggle with.

All this requires true collaboration that comes from higher levels of trust and openness created by cooperative and meaningful relationships. Put simply, successfully leading in the Network Age requires the intentional and systematic development of a more *relational* leadership—leading with Radical Humility. And it is not just me claiming that. There is a growing body of rigorous academic research that points to the benefits of Humble Leadership on employee engagement[11] and satisfaction,[12] turnover,[13] and bottom-line business results.[14]

Building a strong team through more relational leadership has become *the* critical leadership skill. Despite our deeply ingrained and mistaken belief that leaders must be "infallible" heroes (but sometimes turn out to be arrogant jerks), we can all learn the skills of leading with humility. My goal is to teach you how.

## That Sounds All Good So Far, But . . .

Despite having made what I believe to be a strong case for humble leadership, you might still have doubts. Let me address three of the most frequently asked questions I get asked about humble leadership.

### What If My Team Member Feels Uncomfortable Sharing and Deepening Our Relationship?

You must strike a balance between respecting other people's boundaries and encouraging them to open up if you want to develop meaningful relationships at work. This conundrum does not have a one-size-fits-all answer. Assuming too much trust too soon might be a grave error. When you hardly know each other, don't expose your soul and then expect the other person to do the same.

But you have to start somewhere. Start with a one-on-one conversation and push yourself to ask questions that are a little more personal and reveal a little more of yourself than you typically would (within the realm of what is culturally and ethically appropriate, of course). There is no secret recipe for this, so as the conversation progresses, you must trust your instincts. Don't push it if the other person looks reluctant to share. It takes time to build trusted connections.

The depth of relationships with various team members inevitably varies. You will quickly reach a deeply personal level with some team members, and you won't with others. That's OK. Knowing everyone's most private information is not necessary for developing a connection. Leading relationally simply means getting to know the individuals you work with beyond just the function they serve for you. In chapter 6, we will return to this topic in greater detail.

### What If I Work in a Command-and-Control Culture?

Practicing humble leadership in an authoritarian, command-and-control culture is difficult, no doubt. But don't let that discourage you. It is possible to create your own pocket of humility even in highly hierarchical settings.

## Create Your Own Pocket of Humble Leadership Excellence

In the introduction I shared the big and hard questions I grappled with about our role as peacekeepers in Kosovo. I had plenty of doubts. At times I was very unsure about the value we were bringing and how much good we really were doing. I also knew there was little if anything I could do to change the overall setting of our peacekeeping force.

However, what I could directly impact on a daily basis was the leadership of my immediate team. Harvard professor Amy Edmondson, one of the academic authorities on psychological safety whom you will meet in Shift V, calls this "looking down."[15] She points out how we all tend to look up in the direction of the manager above us in the hierarchy. Then we throw up our hands in frustration about our lack of control and ability to change things.

Instead, she points out, we must train ourselves to look in the other direction: down. Create a pocket of humble leadership excellence in your team no matter what those above and around you are doing. This is a realm you have direct say in. Create a culture of relationship building and transparency. Help your team reframe and embrace failure as a natural byproduct of learning and growing. As tennis legend Arthur Ashe said, "Start where you are, use what you have, do what you can."

You can make a difference with and for your team members, and who knows? Your humble leadership might even spread to other parts of your organization.

## "Sir, I Intend To . . ."

Navy Captain David Marquet pulled off an impressive pocket of humble leadership excellence on the multibillion-dollar nuclear-powered submarine USS *Santa Fe*. Having been trained on different ships, he took over the *Santa Fe* not knowing the ship. To make things worse, the crew was dogged with poor morale, lackluster performance, and the worst retention in the fleet.

In his book *Turn the Ship Around! A True Story of Turning Followers into Leaders*,[16] he writes about his failures early in his career and how an increasing self-awareness helped him to learn from them. As a result, with the *Santa Fe*, he was determined to try something new and different from the traditional navy leadership model of the "know-it-all hero" giving top-down orders.

Upon taking over the ship, Marquet immediately started to deepen relationships with his crew by walking around the ship, hanging around his crew members, and asking a lot of questions. He specifically inquired about how they were feeling about the ship and what procedures they wanted to see change. He then started to implement some of these changes in conjunction with his crew, sometimes even breaking navy protocol if it did not make sense.

Marquet masterfully used the power of language to create a pocket of humble leadership excellence on the *Santa Fe*. Two examples stand out:

1. He empowered his crew by changing the way orders were given. For example, instead of a direct report using the slightly submissive "requesting permission to . . . (submerge the ship, increase the speed, etc.)," he insisted that the direct report announce their suggestion in the more empowered form of "Sir, I intend to . . ." to which the officer might ask some clarifying questions and then would respond "Very well" if it made sense.[17] This seemingly small change enhanced initiative and ownership on the crew's part. He also made it safe for his crew to think out loud and question assumptions about proposed decisions. This fostered informal communication and built trust.

2. In the spirit of valuing each crew member as a whole person and not just for the role they were fulfilling, he introduced the "three-name rule."[18] Whenever a crew member saw a visitor on the ship, he would greet them with three names—the visitor's name, his own name, and the ship's name. For example, "Good morning, Commodore Jones. My name is Petty Officer Mattis. Welcome aboard *Santa Fe*." While initially a bit forced, Marquet understood that acting with pride would eventually lead to pride. Importantly, using their own name started to instill pride into who the crew member was as a person and not just into their position.

Marquet's creation of a pocket of humble leadership excellence on the nuclear power submarine *Santa Fe* turned the ship around in a big way. Over the course of one year, the USS *Santa Fe* went from worst to best in class and set records for performance, morale, and retention. Maybe most impressively, turning his ship into a leadership factory (which you will learn about in chapter 9) resulted in a highly disproportionate number of officers from the *Santa Fe* being tapped as submarine commanders over the following decades.[19]

Marquet's impressive example demonstrates how powerful Radical Humility can be for leadership even in highly hierarchical settings.

### What about the Successful Arrogant Jerks?

Exactly no one would call Steve Jobs, former Microsoft CEO Steve Ballmer, former Uber CEO Travis Kalanick, Mark Zuckerberg, or Elon Musk humble—yet these leaders have clearly enjoyed success. Why would I argue that Radical Humility is key to success when there are clearly counterexamples of leaders who run successful organizations but can be commanding, controlling jerks?

Here is my rebuttal: First, let's remember what we are looking at. We simply have some cases where arrogant, top-down leaders achieved success. This correlation between command-and-control leadership and success does not mean there is a causality. In other words, it might be these leaders are successful either because of their leadership approach or (more likely) in spite of it. Further, we don't know what would have happened if the same company were run by a humble leader.

It is possible that the company would have failed under a different style, but I would argue the more likely scenario is it would have been even more successful with a humble leader at its helm. Certainly, other factors may play a bigger role as well: favorable market conditions, a killer product, great timing, or simply luck.

I do concede there are rare genius leaders who can get away with being less humble because they are so incredibly talented. Most people might think of Steve Jobs, who was fired from his first company for his "unmanageable ego."[20] His famous words "Your work is shit" come to mind. Much less celebrated is that Jobs embraced one aspect of humble leadership—namely intellectual humility—exceptionally well. On being wrong, he said, "I don't really care about being right; I just care about success. I don't mind being wrong, and I'll admit that I'm wrong a lot. It doesn't really matter to me too much. What matters to me is that we do the right thing."[21]

This is an important point I discuss in greater depth throughout the book. You must have the humility to want the *best* idea to win, not *your* idea!

Despite displaying intellectual humility, Steve Jobs was of course most certainly not the poster child for humble leadership. So here is the deal I'll make with you: If you are confident that you are a brilliant, rare genius of the caliber of Steve Jobs, then put this book down now. Don't worry about embracing Radical Humility. Email me and say you'd like your money back because there's nothing of value for you in these pages. However, the rest of us mere mortals cannot afford to not dig deep within ourselves to constantly learn and grow.

The truth is, all of us can benefit from developing and growing our people through a more relational, humble kind of leadership that empowers our teams to make smart decisions faster and more independently. Humble leadership helps you to create better products, stronger teams, and a superior organization—and ultimately helps you become a more empathetic person.

Having made the case for leading with Radical Humility, it's now time to preview each of the 5 THEN to NOW Shifts before diving into the first shift.

## 5 THEN to NOW Shifts = Humble Leadership

Figure 2.3 demonstrates how the five (THEN) to (NOW) Shifts tie into and support the three defining dimensions of humble leadership: (1) Self-Knowledge/Growth Mindset, (2) Leading Relationally—Team/Growth Mindset, and (3) Leading Relationally—Organization/Growth Mindset.

1. **Self-Knowledge/Growth Mindset:** Shift I
2. **Lead Relationally (Team)/Growth Mindset:** Shift II, Shift III, Shift IV
3. **Lead Relationally (Organization)/Growth Mindset:** Shift V

## Figure 2.3: How the 5 THEN to NOW Leadership Shifts Tie into Humble Leadership

| DIMENSIONS | | THEN | NOW |
|---|---|---|---|
| Self-Knowledge/ Growth Mindset | SHIFT I DIG DEEP | Blind spot / Trying to do it all / Personal failure as a loss | Self-awareness / Laser-sharp focus / Failing successfully |
| Leading Relationally (Team)/ Growth Mindset | SHIFT II TOUGH ON RESULTS, TENDER ON PEOPLE | Transactional relationships at work / Feedback that tears down | Strong personal relationships at work / Feedback that builds up |
| | SHIFT III LEAD LIKE A COMPASS | Micromanagement / Talent shortage | Front-line empowerment / Talent magnet |
| | SHIFT IV FULL TRANSPARENCY | False hero, knows-it-all façade / Avoidance, secrecy | Trust through vulnerability / Openness, honesty |
| Leading Relationally (Org.)/ Growth Mindset | SHIFT V CHAMPION A FEARLESS CULTURE | Afraid to speak up; hide, cover up mistakes / Fear-driven culture | Psychological safety / Fearless culture |

HUMBLE LEADERSHIP = NOW LEADERSHIP

Here is a quick preview of the 5 Shifts that, when applied, will help you transform into a humble leader:

# SHIFT I: DIG DEEP

*From Blind Spots (THEN) to Self-Awareness (NOW)*

Leading with Radical Humility requires digging deep within yourself. It requires you to become more self-aware, apply a laser-sharp focus on what really matters, and reframe your failures as growth opportunities.

## SHIFT II: TOUGH ON RESULTS, TENDER ON PEOPLE
*From Heavy-Handed (THEN) to High-Touch, High Standards (NOW)*

Leading with Radical Humility is conveying to your team, "I value you as a whole person and not just as a subordinate who gets things done for me." Radically humble leadership is building trusting and cooperative relationships with your people *while at the same* time holding them to the highest standards.

## SHIFT III: LEAD LIKE A COMPASS
*From Micromanaging (THEN) to Empowerment (NOW)*

Radically humble leadership is parking your ego at the door, getting out of the way, and empowering your teams to make fast decisions independently.

## SHIFT IV: FULL TRANSPARENCY
*From Secrecy and Avoidance (THEN) to Transparency and Openness (NOW)*

Leading with Radical Humility is building trust with your people by appropriately sharing your shortcomings with vulnerability. As you build trust, you can share more about your intentions and goals so that your teams become better at executing independently.

## SHIFT V: CHAMPION A FEARLESS CULTURE
*From Afraid to Speak Up (THEN) to Fearless Culture (NOW)*

Humble organizational leadership requires you to understand and drive the interpersonal and group dynamics of your teams versus simply excelling at your own individual leadership skills. As a humble leader, you know how to transform your teams into high-performing, fearless units where everybody feels safe to speak up and contribute. Humble leadership is driving your teams toward a culture of psychological safety. It means you champion a fearless culture.

Scan the QR code below to get an online version of the 5 THEN to NOW Leadership Shifts that you can print out to post where you can see them every day. Take notes and follow along as we start to build the 5 Shifts together.

# RADICAL HUMILITY

## (THEN) to (NOW)

The following chart captures what Radical Humility is not (THEN) and what it is (NOW). Consider it your cheat sheet that summarizes the main concepts we have covered so far. I will revisit and build upon this table at the end of each Shift so you will have a dynamic snapshot of our progress together as the book builds. By the end, we'll have a concise one-page summary of what you need NOW in your leadership journey.

| What Radical Humility Is Not (THEN) | What Radical Humility Is (NOW) |
| :---: | :---: |
| Insecure | Confident |
| Indifferent | Ambitious |
| Wavering | Decisive |
| Hero leader: I know | Learning leader: good at not knowing |
| Individual wins | Team wins |
| I tell | I ask |

# DIMENSIONS

| | |
|---|---|
| **Self-Knowledge/ Growth Mindset** | ## SHIFT I DIG DEEP |

| | |
|---|---|
| **Leading Relationally (Team)/ Growth Mindset** | ## SHIFT II TOUGH ON RESULTS, TENDER ON PEOPLE |
| | ## SHIFT III LEAD LIKE A COMPASS |
| | ## SHIFT IV FULL TRANSPARENCY |

| | |
|---|---|
| **Leading Relationally (Org.)/ Growth Mindset** | ## SHIFT V CHAMPION A FEARLESS CULTURE |

|  **THEN**  |  **NOW**  |
|---|---|

| Blind spot | Self-awareness |
| Trying to do it all | Laser-sharp focus |
| Personal failure as a loss | Failing successfully |

| Transactional relationships at work | Strong personal relationships at work |
| Feedback that tears down | Feedback that builds up |

| Micromanagement | Front-line empowerment |
| Talent shortage | Talent magnet |

| False hero, knows-it-all façade | Trust through vulnerability |
| Avoidance, secrecy | Openness, honesty |

| Afraid to speak up; hide, cover up mistakes | Psychological safety |
| Fear-driven culture | Fearless culture |

**HUMBLE LEADERSHIP = NOW LEADERSHIP**

# SHIFT I
# DIG DEEP

## Humbly Ask Yourself the Big Questions:

1. How do you become more self-aware?
2. How do you make time and energy for what really matters?
3. How do you embrace failure for personal growth?

Leading with Radical Humility requires digging deep to know how best to leverage your strengths and talents for your team while honestly owning your shortcomings and working to improve them. This sounds obvious, but it's not enough to understand yourself. You must also commit to putting change into action. Tips and strategies found in this Shift will help you apply what you learn when you dig deep.

To be a humble leader, you must be self-aware, focus with intention on what really matters, and reframe your failures as growth opportunities.

In this Shift, you will learn (1) why knowing thyself is key to your success as a leader. You will master the practical steps you can take with your team to develop a more accurate view of yourself that is in line with how others see you, all with the goal of reducing your blind spots. You will then learn how to implement the research-backed, proven Stakeholder Centered Coaching® process I have applied with hundreds of leaders to help you become a more effective leader.

In this Shift, you will also learn (2) that, much like an elite athlete, you can achieve almost *anything* you put your mind to, but you must have the humility to know that you cannot do *everything*. Being busy and being productive are not the same thing. When you go against the social grain that celebrates busyness as a badge of honor, you discover you can say no. Here, you will learn practical tools to free up time and energy for what really matters.

Finally, in this Shift, you will learn (3) how to fail successfully and model it for your people. I will guide you through my biggest athletic failure, which almost cost me my life, and demonstrate the emotional and intellectual road I traveled to come back stronger.

# CHAPTER 3
## KNOW THYSELF

*Don't accept your dog's admiration as conclusive*
*evidence that you are wonderful.*
**—Ann Landers**

## How Do You Become More Self-Aware?

"Please have a seat," my boss said, then closed the door behind her.

I sat down slowly, feeling a little concerned at how serious she was.

"Urs, there's no easy way to put this, but we are letting you go, effective immediately. You have thirty minutes to gather your belongings. Please hand me your badge."

I was in shock. I quietly packed my belongings, and a half hour later, I stepped out of the office lobby into the bright sunlight of the busy streets of downtown Seattle wondering what to do next. In the blink of an eye, my attempt at transitioning from independent leadership consultant to marketing director at an investment management firm had come to a screeching halt.

So, what happened?

I was almost two years into my job as marketing director at my former executive coaching client's firm. While I did not have a marketing background, I was getting up to speed on things quickly. I drove my team (and my bosses) hard. Before I came in-house, I coached the CEO individually. I also team-coached the three C-executives.

As a result, and to a fault, I was never shy to share my opinion. I was willing to bring up the elephant in the room, be it with my bosses, my peers, or my team. I had strong relationships with many folks at the firm. Many remained friends over the years, and to this day, I am still a client. My team was loyal, and they made a point of regularly sharing how much they appreciated having me as their boss.

But a week earlier, I attended a cost-cutting meeting with my three bosses: the CEO, COO, and CFO. It was 2008, and the stock market kept tanking. As a result, the revenue of the firm was evaporating before our eyes. We already had three painful rounds of layoffs behind us.

The meeting was just about to wrap up when I turned to the three C-level executives and said, "Well, for a firm our size, I really don't think we need three C-levels; I think one would do."

The stunned look on the faces of my three bosses told me I might have gone too far this time. At that moment, I overplayed my strength of speaking my mind and turned it into a huge liability.

I am not proud to repeat it now. No question; I have learned my lessons. But at that moment, I lacked the self-awareness to show up productively. And just to be clear, I am not advocating for playing office politics and being afraid to speak up. The content of my message was on target, but I was too impulsive with my comment and made a poor choice about the timing and delivery of my message. The company was in dire financial straits, and I made myself a simple target by not knowing when to shut up. It cost me my job.

It's like I often say: "Growth lies behind door number discomfort." In my case, this was literally true once my boss closed that door behind me.

Knowing thyself, as the ancient Greeks knew, means developing better self-awareness about your strengths and weaknesses. It means having an accurate view of yourself, your talents, and your achievements as well as your shortcomings.

Importantly, as a self-aware leader, you should assess your strengths and weaknesses in line with how others see you. There is a solid body of empirical research demonstrating that leaders with greater self-awareness make better decisions, build stronger relationships, and communicate more effectively. They are more likely to get promoted, and their companies are more profitable.[1]

## Looking through the Johari Window

One of the main goals of knowing thyself is to discover your blind spots. The Johari window (figure 3.1) is a helpful model to help you do just that. It was created in 1955 by psychologists Joseph Luft and Harrington Ingham (Jo + Hari = JoHari).[2]

*Figure 3.1: The Johari Window*

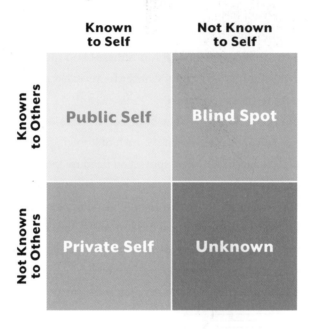

The top left quadrant is the Public Self. It encompasses the things I know about myself and the things I am comfortable sharing with others. Examples might include where I grew up, my current job, or how and where I spent my last vacation.

The bottom left quadrant holds the things I conceal from others, my Private Self. These are things I don't feel comfortable revealing because I feel embarrassed about them. Examples might be a bad mistake that cost my previous employer a lot of money, a bad breakup, or an illness or addiction. This quadrant also includes things I don't share with others because I fear it would be hurtful to reveal to their face.

The bottom right is the Unknown. Neither you nor I nor others can know them. An example might be your lack of knowledge about how many learnings from this book you will be implementing with your team over the next month. (I sure would like to think there would be plenty! But at the moment, no one knows.)

The top right quadrant is most interesting for us as humble leaders. These are my Blind Spots: things everyone else knows about me but I do not. It can be anything from how I dress, my demeanor, my body language, what I say, and how and when I say it.

One of the ironies of social interactions is these blind spots are well known by everybody around you but might never be revealed to you unless you take active steps to make it happen.

When you take action to reduce your blind spots, you increase your self-awareness. You go further down the path of knowing thyself, of digging deep within. To reduce your blind spots, you need to apply ambition, confidence, and decisiveness.

As a humble leader, you have the *ambition* to discover your blind spots. You want to learn about them so you can improve upon them. As a humble leader, you have the *confidence* to hear the hard truth about what others really think of you. And lastly, as a humble leader, you know that despite all your strengths and talents, there are always plenty of things you can improve, and you take *decisive* action to get better.

## Conduct a 360 Survey

The most effective tool to discover your blind spots is a 360-degree feedback survey, or "360" for short (figure 3.2). A 360 asks *everyone* (hence, 360) around you what you do well and what you should improve. Direct reports, peers, bosses, customers . . . everyone is a possible survey taker for your 360. It is a must-use tool in leadership development, and I have administered well over a hundred 360s myself.

In the absence of a formal 360, you can conduct an informal 360 yourself. Seek out people whom you interact with regularly and ask them for feedback on how you are doing as a leader. Seek out your "loving critics," people who have your best interests at heart and can be brutally honest with you. Simply ask them the following:

- What do I do well as a manager?
- What could I do better as a manager?

Alternatively, you can use the Start, Stop, Continue framework. Ask them:

- What should I start doing?
- What should I stop doing?
- What should I continue doing?

For tips on how to make it safe for your direct reports to give you honest feedback, see the "NOW Leadership . . . NOW! Soliciting Honest Feedback" prompt at the end of this section.

# NOW Leadership … NOW!

## *Schedule Your 360*

Make a list of the people you will conduct your informal 360 with. Make sure you cover the full 360 (manager, peers, direct reports). Then reach out and set up a thirty-minute meeting with each of them.

1. _____
2. _____
3. _____
4. _____
5. _____
6. _____
7. _____
8. _____

If you have specific areas you are working on, such as delegating, empowering, or follow-through, you want to especially inquire about those. Ask the question, then simply listen, take notes, and thank them. Never defend, justify, or argue with the person. You are simply here to ask, listen, and humbly learn about how others see you.

You might fear that asking for feedback will make you look flawed or lacking in confidence. I hate to break it to you, but your team already knows you are not perfect. Asking for feedback does not make you appear weak. The opposite is true. Genuinely soliciting feedback builds trust and deepens relationships. If you feel self-conscious about asking for feedback, here is what I often tell my clients: leadership is not a popularity contest. You always ask, you always listen, you always thank, but *you* get to decide if and how you act on the feedback.

Gathering feedback from your team takes guts, but don't stop there. Many organizations administer 360s for their team members but then stop the process too early. While it is no doubt useful to receive the data from your

360, it is unlikely that you will be able to make meaningful changes to your leadership simply by having the feedback in hand. Stopping once you receive the 360 feedback is like administering a fitness assessment and then expecting people to start working out simply because they have the results.

The data is very clear. To make meaningful changes, you need to follow a process that includes having a regular check-in with your team members. Leadership never happens in a vacuum. Executive coaching guru Marshall Goldsmith pioneered the practice of involving your team (or stakeholders) in your leadership development. He showed in a large quantitative study across eleven thousand leaders on four continents that involving your stakeholders in your development process is a key success factor in making meaningful change.[3]

I have used Goldsmith's Stakeholder Centered Coaching® almost exclusively over the course of the last fifteen years with close to a 100 percent success rate of meaningful change by the client. The approach differs from other executive coaching in two important ways:

1. It includes regular follow-up with stakeholders.
2. It asks not only for feedback, which by definition is backward-looking, but also for suggestions for the future—feed*forward*.

Even if you do not work with a coach, you can include your team members (or stakeholders) in your process of getting better, thereby vastly improving your chances of making meaningful change to your leadership.

Figure 3.3 summarizes the Stakeholder Centered Coaching® process I am about to take you through:

*Figure 3.3: Stakeholder Centered Coaching® Process, Step by Step*

| Conduct Informal 360-Degree Survey | Choose and Invite Stakeholders | Hold Stakeholders Kickoff Meeting | Conduct Monthly Check-In Meetings with Stakeholders |
|---|---|---|---|
| 1 on 1 meetings, 30 min | 1 on 1 meetings, 5 min | Meeting of all Stakeholders, 15 min | Feedback and Feedforward, 1 on 1 meetings, 15 min |

# NOW Leadership ... NOW!
## Soliciting Honest Feedback

Use the strategies in the right column to make your direct reports feel safe to give you honest feedback.[4]

| Obstacle to honest feedback from your direct reports | What to do and say |
| --- | --- |
| **Worried that giving you critical feedback could threaten their career prospects** | Demonstrate Radical Humility by saying something like, *"I know that it can feel uncomfortable to give feedback to your boss. I had the same concerns with my boss. Let me reassure you that I see your willingness to give me honest and helpful feedback—even if it's negative—as one of your professional strengths."* <br><br> Frame feedback as helping you to achieve a commitment you've made to yourself. Then ask for help meeting your commitment. Say: *"Would you please help by giving me feedback on the commitment I've made to myself?"* That way, your direct report can view their feedback as helping you make good on a promise you've made to yourself. |
| **Worried about hurting their relationship with you** | Demonstrate your self-awareness by taking the lead in giving yourself constructive feedback first, which can mitigate their fears. Say something like, *"I know that I tend to move at a fast pace, often forgetting that not everybody does. Others have shared with me that they find it hard when I don't take the time to get everybody on board with my decisions. I'd like to get better at that. Would you share what you've experienced?"* And then, once you have them talking, you can ask, *"And is there anything else I could be working to improve that would make your work easier?"* |

## Choose and Invite Stakeholders

Who should your stakeholders be, and how many should you choose? To get a wide variety of input, you want to include your direct reports, your boss, a couple of peers, and some important people outside your department (e.g., human resources, finance) and/or outside your organization (e.g., clients, vendors). There will be overlap between the people you surveyed for your 360 and your stakeholders.

Between eight and fifteen is a good number (see figure 3.4). It is important that you choose stakeholders who interact with you on a regular basis so they will be able to provide meaningful feedback on the changes you are working on. Don't choose only your fan club. Aim for a wide variety of people, including those you have challenges working with. Ask them to be honest, direct, and constructive with you.

I also encourage my clients to include a personal stakeholder such as a spouse or family member. This might sound strange, but some clients have told me the behavioral change they undertook was most felt and appreciated by their personal relationships. You might think you are a different person at work than at home. The reality is, your strengths and weaknesses follow you regardless of context—whether you like it or not. The upside, of course, is that any positive change you are making in your leadership at work will have a positive spillover effect at home.

*Figure 3.4: Your Stakeholder Checklist*

- ✅ 8–15 people
- ✅ Interact with you on a regular basis
- ✅ Willing to give you feedback and feedforward once per month for 15 minutes
- ✅ Mix of people: not only your fan club, include folks you find challenging
- ✅ Must be honest and constructive
- ✅ Include a personal stakeholder

# NOW Leadership... NOW
## Choosing Your Stakeholders

Make a list of the people who you will invite to be your stakeholders.

1. _____
2. _____
3. _____
4. _____
5. _____
6. _____
7. _____
8. _____

## Hold a Stakeholder Kickoff Meeting

After setting your goals based on the 360 (either a formal one or your own informal one) and choosing and inviting your stakeholders, hold a brief stakeholder kickoff meeting. This will take about fifteen minutes. To make it easy, you can do this at the end of your regular team meeting and invite your boss, your peers, and the external stakeholders to that portion of your team meeting. Thank them for the feedback in the 360 and briefly share the strengths communicated to you in it. These are the bright spots. Then present the goals you want to improve upon. Focus on no more than three.

The simple act of standing up in front of your stakeholders and communicating your developmental goals is humbling. It requires guts. By explicitly sharing your goals, you communicate to your team that while you have wonderful strengths, you are by no means perfect and are looking at getting better. In the process you demonstrate, yes ... Radical Humility and vulnerability ... in front of your team, which is one of the most powerful ways to build and deepen trust.

To give you an idea of what you could work on, here is a list of some of the most common goals of my clients:

- become a better listener
- treat others with more respect
- listen to other points of view with an open mind before giving an opinion
- empower and develop the team
- build strong, collaborative partnerships across the organization
- become more assertive
- drive more aggressive business results
- embrace conflict; be willing to say no
- become more decisive
- seek input from a broader group before making decisions
- express more recognition and direct feedback
- be more visible and accessible
- improve prioritizing and delegating under pressure
- mentor and delegate to teammates effectively

## Gather Feedback and Feedforward

For many of us, feedback has a negative connotation. We associate it with judgment and criticism, and we often resist giving and receiving it. Yet we know this to be true: the strongest leaders are feedback magnets with the humility and confidence to constantly seek input on how they can do better.[5]

Proactively asking for feedback sends a strong signal about your willingness to improve. Once you start to train the feedback muscle, it becomes much easier over time. The most successful leaders I have worked alongside during my career are consistently asking for feedback and approach leadership with a learning mindset. No matter how successful they are, they always strive to get better. As one of my all-time favorite CEO clients puts it: "Why do we look back? To learn. Because to win, we must outlearn the competition."

While feedback focuses on the past, feedforward provides suggestions for the future (table 3.1). What does asking for feedforward look like? It might sound something like this: "Hi, Barbara. I want to become a better listener. What concrete ideas and suggestions do you have for me to become a better listener?"

Table 3.1: Feedback vs. Feedforward

| Feedback | Feedforward |
| --- | --- |
| Assessing the past | Suggestions for the future |
| Judgment (good, bad) | No judgment, only suggestions |
| Can be hard to give and receive | Easy to give and receive |
| Look back to learn | Look ahead to do better |
| Best when specific and behavioral | Best when specific and behavioral |

What you are after are behavioral ideas and suggestions that you can implement right away and start to do differently now and in the future. Valuable feedforward for becoming a better listener might be "Don't interrupt. Put your cell phone away during meetings. Make eye contact. Watch your body language. Paraphrase what you heard me say."

As you solicit feedforward from your stakeholders, you compile a list of all the suggestions and then decide which ones you want to focus on. Again, in the spirit of focus, I strongly suggest you pick one to three feedforward items for each of your coaching goals.

Because feedforward is future-oriented, it is a hugely powerful tool. It provides you with a blueprint on how to get better, starting tomorrow.

And one more thing: People love being asked for advice. By asking your stakeholders to provide feedforward, you make it clear you value their ideas and suggestions, and in the process you implicitly make them part of your journey to becoming a better leader.

## Regular Follow-Up with Stakeholders

After the initial stakeholder kickoff meeting where you brought everyone together, follow up with your stakeholders individually every month. These very brief (fifteen minutes or less) check-in meetings have two parts.

During the first part, ask for feedback on the progress you've made toward your coaching goal. This sounds something like, "As you know, I have been working on becoming a better listener. I especially have been working on not interrupting and paraphrasing. How have I been doing the last month?" Then you shut up and listen.

The second part of the stakeholder check-in meeting is the solicitation of feedforward. Something along the lines of "Thank you for your feedback. I really appreciate it. What other concrete ideas do you have for me that I can implement to become a better listener?" Again, what you are looking for here is a list of concrete behavioral suggestions.

By following up monthly with stakeholders, you take active steps to shape how you are perceived. It is incredibly difficult to shape perception—often much harder than making the actual behavioral change—because we all suffer from confirmation bias. For example, if I believe you are a poor delegator, I will unconsciously look for information that confirms my belief. You can delegate nine times perfectly and slip the tenth time, and I will say, "See, I knew it. She is a poor delegator." By following up regularly, you start to shape perception.

Occasionally I sense skepticism at the onset of coaching engagements. Even though stakeholders do not come right out and say it, they have reservations about the client's ability to make meaningful changes. As the first monthly check-in comes around, the stakeholders are positively surprised the person is following up.

The second month rolls around, and now they start to think, "Wow, Anna is actually serious about this." Perception starts to shift month over month. By consistently following up and seeking feedback and feedforward from the people who count, you shape perception.

An important side benefit of these follow-up meetings is they can help change the quality of conversations inside your organization. These check-ins are all about humble improvement and getting better. In many cases, the stakeholder sees you successfully working on your goal and becomes motivated to themselves pick something to get better at. The check-in meetings then become a two-way feedback and feedforward meeting that is focused on supporting each other to get better. The tone spreads through the organization.

While the vast majority of your work in better knowing thyself involves interacting with your stakeholders, I strongly suggest you also engage in some introspection.

## Introspection: Write a Daily Journal

Journaling is a simple yet powerful way to dive deep within yourself to reflect and improve your self-awareness. When you write down your thoughts and feelings, you externalize them and quite literally offload them onto your pages.

By creating that distance, you become a more objective observer of yourself. Plenty of highly successful leaders swear by journaling, from former US president Barack Obama to Sir Richard Branson. Start by buying a real physical journal. Writing digitally doesn't provide the same benefits as writing by hand. Writing in a physical journal is a tactile experience. It forces you to peel yourself away from the screens we are all so attached to during the daily grind. Writing in a physical journal also allows you more freedom to choose where you want to write, which also gets you out of your routine.

## NOW Leadership ... NOW!
### *Kick-Start Your Journaling Habit*

Carve out fifteen minutes, preferably the same time every day, and journal whatever comes to mind. If you are unsure how to get started, use these trigger questions:

How am I feeling about my leadership right now?

_____

_____

What three things have I done well over the last twenty-four hours?

1. _____
2. _____
3. _____

What three things do I want to improve?

1. _____
2. _____
3. _____

What is my top priority in my business and life?

_____

## Humble Leadership Is a Contact Sport

If all this transparent feedback and feedforward check-in with your stakeholders talk sounds a bit scary to you, you are not alone. Humble leadership requires a commitment to know thyself. To get there, there is no way around engaging your team members. It requires you to park your ego at the door by putting yourself out there and humbly asking for input and owning your weaknesses.

As you know by now, humble leadership is not for the weak of heart, and it's not soft. Humble leadership is a contact sport that requires you to be in the ring, getting bruised and even knocked down occasionally. With a 360, you quite literally are asking to get it from all sides. The good news is that the payoff is huge. When you involve your team in your journey of getting to know thyself, you are taking the road less traveled by most—but a path great leaders are willing to walk.

# CHAPTER 4
## FOCUS LIKE AN ELITE ATHLETE

*If you want something new, you have to stop something old.*
**—Peter Drucker**

### How Do You Make Time and Energy for What Really Matters?

This photo shows me racing at the Winter World University Games in Zakopane, Poland, in 1993. It's the 4x10km relay, and I am racing the first leg. This is the last steep climb before the transition to the second racer.

Here's a rhetorical question for you: How many different things am I thinking about at this moment?

The answer, of course, is one. One: razor-sharp focus on staying with the French guy right in front of me because those few feet between him and me right now are the difference between a bronze medal and going home empty-handed. My lungs burn, my whole body is on fire, and I am most certainly not thinking about my studies, my grades, my girlfriend, my to-do list, or what I am going to do with my life after graduation. I am hyper-focused on moving into third place until I hand off to the second Swiss skier of our relay team (which I am proud to say I did).

Successful athletes are masters at focusing and compartmentalizing. We make a choice to devote ourselves passionately to our craft and being the best we can possibly be at it. Greg Searle, Olympic gold medalist in rowing, said it well: "I never made any sacrifices; I made choices."[1]

The incredible focus that elite athletes display in search of victory is a wonderful metaphor for what is needed to lead with humility. As a humble leader, you know you can achieve almost *anything* you put your mind to, but you have the humility to know you cannot do *everything*.

Humble leadership does not mean adding more to your to-do list. In fact, it might mean taking things off it and stopping doing things that distract from what's actually important. I strongly believe that many people don't achieve what they want to because they spread themselves too thin. Try to do too much at the same time, and you end up not doing anything particularly well. The solution? Razor-sharp focus. Eliminate. Stop doing things that don't get you closer to your goal.

I sometimes get pushback with the concept of stopping doing things when I talk about it in my keynote speeches.

"How can I do less when I am in the process of building a business?"

"How can I stop doing things when my people are so overwhelmed?"

I get it. It's challenging. When you are just barely holding it together to make ends meet, "stop doing things" can feel out of touch. Yet here is my challenge to you: Even (and especially) if you feel you have no choice, even if you are feeling incredibly busy just trying to bring in enough cash or keep the lights on, the concept of singular focus is worthwhile.

Take an honest look at how you spend your time and energy. It will help you identify which activities provide the most value . . . and which ones are a drain on resources. The well-known Pareto principle (also known as the 80/20 rule), for example, states that 80 percent of your results come from 20 percent of your activities (or that 80 percent of your revenue comes from 20 percent of your clients).

When you feel you have no choice but to stay on the treadmill, the exercise of identifying and eliminating low-value-add activities can in fact be extremely helpful. It's worth reminding yourself that if you are not getting everything on your to-do list accomplished each day, you are already not doing things. Deciding to stop doing certain things is simply taking control of the process rather than living in the chaos of being overwhelmed.

An honest assessment will give you time and energy to double down on those activities that yield the highest results. The big quandary to me is how most of us recognize the clear value of sharp focus, saying no, and doing less, yet the vast majority of us really suck at it. Why is that?

## Are You Busy, or Are You Productive?

My plea goes utterly against the grain of our mainstream culture, where being "busy" is often equated with being important and productive. As a society we are addicted to busyness; it is a badge of honor.

Just think about how we introduce ourselves at networking events or cocktail parties.

"Hi, I am Urs. How are you?"

"Hi, I'm Carol."

"Nice to meet you, Carol. What do you do?"

"Nice to meet you, too, Urs. I run a staffing agency in Chicago."

"How is that going for you?"

"I am super busy."

And how do I respond?

"That's great! You are busy. Better than the other way around!"

What counts, of course, is results, not staying busy. Busyness is the antithesis of focus. To be the most effective professionals and leaders, we need to focus—and that requires the humility to eliminate nonessentials.

Eliminating things from your life is hard because it means saying no to something or somebody. As humans we naturally want to be liked, and we want to please. Saying no means pushing against the social grain. It requires courage and mental and emotional discipline to do it well.

My keynote speaker colleague Jeremiah Brown won an Olympic silver medal as a member of the Canadian eight-man rowing team at the London 2012 Olympic Games. Pretty impressive, right? But what is truly amazing about Jeremiah is that four years before winning the Olympic medal, he had *never* even tried rowing (and he was also a young father at that time). Jeremiah is one of very few Olympians ever to have started learning his sport only four years before winning a medal at the Olympics.[2] His secret? You've probably already guessed it: focus and saying no to all distractions.

I don't have to look any further than my own family to find a similar example. My sister Vroni, in the photo below, is a three-time orienteering world champion with numerous silver and bronze medals at world and European championships to her name. "When I train or race, I go through the mental exercise of putting all the distractions of my busy life aside," Vroni said. "For the duration of the race or training, I commit to be an athlete *and only* an athlete. Not a mother, not a wife, not a math teacher, only a highly focused athlete who is in it to win."

For twenty years she competed at the highest level of her sport before transitioning to coaching, where she led the Swiss women's team to world-class dominance and now is en route to doing the same with the Finnish team. Two years after her retirement, she ran a sub-three-hour marathon at age forty-two, after having four wonderful daughters. One of the main secrets of her success aside from an incredible work ethic and drive?

Laser focus and eliminating all distractions before and during every training session and race.

Can you tell I am a little proud of my younger sister?

# NOW Leadership ... NOW!

## The 4 Ds of Your To-Do List

Go through your to-do list, and assign each item to one of these categories. Ask yourself for every item:

1. **D**elegate. Who else can and should do this? My items that I will delegate are _____

2. **D**rop. What do I need to stop doing? My items that I will drop are

   _____

3. **D**efer. What can I do later? (To free your mind from thinking and worrying about it, put a date on your calendar—defer it—for when you will revisit this item.) My items that I will defer are

   _____

4. **D**o. What do I need to do? (This item is on you. Only you can do it. So ... do it! As the president of a branding firm once told me, a bit tongue in cheek: "The best way of getting things done is ... doing them.") The items that I will do are _____

   _____

## Cleaning Out Your Time-Management Closet

What if you adopted the mindset of elite athletes? What if you stopped celebrating being busy as a measure of how important you are? What if you moved from pursuing more to pursuing less ... but doing it better?

Google gets it. Every time a project gets discontinued at Google, it's a reason to celebrate. Why? Someone had the humility and guts to make a hard decision and kill a project, and as a result, resources are freed up. But

Google takes the concept a step further. At killedbygoogle.com, you find a eulogy for every product, app, and service that Google has ruthlessly killed (288 and counting).

Remember, for example, the Google glasses? They were two years old when they were eliminated in 2015 in one of the more public business flops of recent memory. There were plenty of privacy and security concerns that led to users being "glassholes" (which may be a clear sign that it's time to move on from a bad idea).

Greg McKeown, in his outstanding *New York Times* bestseller *Essentialism: The Disciplined Pursuit of Less*,[3] identifies three mindsets that will help you focus and say no so you have time and energy for what really matters.

1. Individual choice: Even if it does not seem like it at times, you have a lot more choice about how you spend your energy and time than you think.
   **We must move from "We have to" to "We choose to."**

2. Lots of noise: Almost everything is noise, and very few things are exceptionally valuable. Because some things are so much more important, it is worth the effort to identify them.
   **We must move from "It's all important" to "Only a few things really matter."**

3. Trade-offs are real: We cannot have or do it all. Instead of asking, "How can I make it all work?" ask, "Which problem do I want to solve?"
   **We must move from "I can do both" to "I can do almost anything but not everything."**

Once you adopt these mindsets, you evaluate your existing and new projects and activities in a whole new way. It can be liberating. Be ruthless. Think of this process as cleaning out your time-management closet. When you clean out your closet, instead of asking, "Will I ever wear this?" ask, "Do I really love it? Does it look great on me? Do I wear it frequently?"[4] If the answer is no to one of these questions, get rid of it. The same goes for your activities and to-dos in your personal and work life. Ask yourself, "Will this activity or effort make the highest possible contribution toward my goal?"

## The Stop-Doing List

The stop-doing list is a very simple tool that can help you free up time. What might go on it? Simple tasks that you can outsource or automate. Unproductive behaviors. Things you do out of habit or guilt. For inspiration, here is my personal stop-doing list.

### Urs's Stop-Doing List

- **Personal**
    - Garden upkeep, cutting the grass (outsourced)
    - Cleaning (outsourced)
    - Being involved in more than one volunteer activity at any time

- **Unproductive Behaviors**
    - Checking my phone when I am with my boys
    - Drinking alcohol daily
    - Training through injuries

- **Business**
    - Constant email checking (instead, check just twice per day, respond once per day)
    - Doing social media myself (outsourced)
    - Trying to have more than two areas to focus on at any time

## NOW Leadership ... NOW!
### *The Stop-Doing List*

Commit to one thing in your personal life and one thing in your work life that you will stop doing. Write it down and share the personal item with your family and the professional item with your colleagues at work.

My stop-doing item at home: _____

My stop-doing item at work: _____

## Be Ruthless in Detecting Value

Many of us fall into the trap of continuing the same old activities and efforts, then adding a new one without eliminating anything. This is bad math and bad practice ... and it will catch up to you. We do this out of habit, sometimes out of intellectual laziness, fear, or guilt about pushing back.

Melissa, one of my coaching clients, understands this trap well. When her boss approaches her with a new project, a new to-do, she looks at her calendar and responds: "I have four unscheduled hours between now and then. If this requires more than four hours, let's talk about which other task I should not being doing instead." Melissa takes responsibility for and control of how she spends her time and energy. Remember, you have more choice than you think. If you don't prioritize your to-dos, someone else will.

You must exert the discipline to systematically explore and evaluate your options before committing to any. Be ruthless in distinguishing, as McKeown put it, "the vital few options from the trivial many."[5]

What if you became committed to identifying and evaluating which 20 percent of your effort produces 80 percent of your results? Which 20 percent produces the most revenue, makes you most effective as a leader, or makes you happiest? Identify the 20 percent, and then double down on those efforts. Kill the rest. McKeown's *Essentialism* reminds us that we live in a world where almost everything is worthless and few things are exceptionally valuable. Why wouldn't you treasure and protect those things?

---

## NOW Leadership ... NOW!
### *Don't Just Do Something, Sit There*

When evaluating new activities and projects, use the questions that follow as criteria. Pursue them only if you can answer all three questions with a resounding *yes*:

- Do I truly have my heart in this? (passion) Yes? No? _____
- Am I at my best doing it? (talent) Yes? No? _____
- Does this generate positive results for me or my team? (outcome) Yes? No? _____

If it's not a clear *yes* on all three, then don't just do something, sit there.

---

## How Your WHY Helps You Focus

Over the past few years, I had the privilege of coaching several special operators such as Navy SEALs, Green Berets, and Army Rangers on their transition from military service into the business world. Part of their transition journey includes the drafting of a personal WHY statement—a personal WHY is a concise statement that identifies your core purpose, values, and priorities in life.

I am always amazed how these hardcore, no-nonsense warriors dive into their life stories. They share with vulnerability and humility where they came from and how they became who they are today. It's uncomfortable and unfamiliar territory for most of them. Yet they tackle this seemingly soft and touchy-feely requirement with gusto and enthusiasm.

They come out the other end with a WHY statement that becomes their North Star as they navigate their journey from special operator to business leader.

Here are two examples of personal WHY statements of special operators I received permission to share:

"I serve as a leader by encouraging innovative ideas and forward thinking so that my team can create health-care solutions that will improve the lives of others."

"To help others discover the greatest version of themselves, so that together we can live to our highest potential and inspire others to do the same."

And here is mine: "I am living an adventurous, passionate, and healthy life by accomplishing ambitious, intense, and unconventional projects that make a difference in the world. I build deep, meaningful relationships and enjoy a well-deserved sense of well-being."

How do *you* identify what you should focus on? A concise personal WHY statement that provides clear guardrails for what you should and should not be focusing your time and energy on is the critical first step. Defining your WHY statement forces you to dig deep into yourself, your values, and what truly drives you.

Drafting your WHY statement will help you decide which projects and goals you should pursue, and equally important, which ones to let go of. It can make saying no to options that do not align with your WHY statement much easier.

My service as a peacekeeper, athletic endeavors, and keynote speaking, as well as writing this book, very clearly align with my mission statement. (Right now, I am finding that writing this book is a particularly "ambitious" project!) Transitioning back into a full-time, traditional corporate role in a large organization, on the other hand, would not be in line with my WHY.

# NOW Leadership ... NOW!

## Draft Your WHY

This simple framework can get you started on your WHY:

"I will _____ (action)

for _____ (audience)

by _____ (skills)

to _____ (desired result)."

Use the following questions to start reflecting on your WHY. Seek out friends, peers, and mentors. Ask them to provide feedback on your current version of your personal mission statement. Then go back and incorporate their input as you finalize your WHY.[6]

1. What is most important to you?
   - Who are you today, and who do you want to become?

     _____

     _____

   - What are you most passionate about? What do you truly love intrinsically?

     _____

     _____

2. What are your most important goals?
   - What does the best version of you look like? In your career and your life?

     _____

     _____

   - What do you want to achieve personally and professionally?

     _____

     _____

3. What legacy do you want to leave?
   - How do you want others to remember you?

   _____

   _____

   - Who and what do you want to support with your skills and abilities?

   _____

   _____

## Adding Goals to Your WHY

The WHY statement is an important start, but your goals that stem from it are where you put meat on the bones.

After having defined the WHY, here is how my very personal process of planning my time and energy—of focusing on what matters most—looks like. Please note that I am not getting into the art and science of goal setting here. There are many excellent sources for doing that,[7] and I trust you will look at those as part of your leadership journey. The purpose of sharing my goals here is to illustrate how each goal needs to feed into a higher-level goal (e.g., a daily goal should relate to a weekly goal, a weekly goal into a monthly goal, a monthly goal into a yearly goal, and an annual goal into a three-year goal) that ultimately feeds into your WHY statement.

### My WHY Statement

"I am living an adventurous, passionate, and healthy life by accomplishing ambitious, intense, and unconventional projects that make a difference in the world. I build deep, meaningful relationships and enjoy a well-deserved sense of well-being."

### Three-Year Goal (by 2026)

- To support my boys in applying and transitioning to college life (". . . build deep, meaningful relationships . . .")
- To build a purpose-driven keynote-speaking business with thirty gigs per year (". . .accomplishing ambitious projects that make a difference in the world . . .")
- To complete three Everesting climbs (29,029 feet nonstop climbs) (". . . intense and adventurous projects . . .")
- Spend six weeks per year visiting family in Europe and/or in the mountains (". . . enjoy a well-deserved sense of well-being . . .")

### 2024 Annual Goals That Are Aligned with My WHY

- Get this book published
- Transform my keynote-speaking business into a purpose-driven business
- Direct sales outreach fine-tuned and yielding gigs
- Develop strong relationships with three speaking bureaus
- Spend four weeks in the Swiss Alps with my boys
- Take spring break off to tour colleges with Luc (my older son)
- Complete one Everesting project

### Monthly Goals That Help Me Achieve Annual Goals

- Complete second draft of two chapters of the book
- Shortlist five worthwhile NGOs I could potentially support with my keynote speaking
- Refine email sales outreach based on learnings from this month
- Spend two weekends skiing with my boys

### Weekly Goals That Help Me Achieve Monthly Goals

- Complete second draft of one chapter of the book

- Shortlist one NGO
- Email sales outreach two hours per day, two networking meetings/zoom
- Six workouts (one two-plus hours, one high intensity, one strength)

### Daily Goals That Help Me Achieve Weekly Goals

- Make myself available for check-in (homework or other) as needed with my boys
- Two hours of sales outreach
- Two hours of writing
- One hour of strength

You get my drift here. All your goals need to eventually support your WHY. Use my examples as an inspiration to set your own yearly, monthly, weekly, and daily goals with a highly disciplined approach of supporting your WHY.

## RIP Toxic Relationships

Apply this same rigor to relationships, and you will be amazed at how much more time you'll create on your schedule and how much more energy you'll have. Most of us have at least one relationship that is ripe for discontinuation. Some people are "energy vampires" who drain your energy and time. If your primary motivation for seeing a person is a sense of obligation or guilt, that relationship is a clear candidate for the chopping block.

When you identify toxic relationships and put them on the stop-seeing list, you have more time and energy for the people in your life who energize you. This, of course, is easier said than done. Eliminating people from your life is difficult. It means confronting somebody and going against a natural tendency of wanting to be liked. But there is no way around it if you are to act honestly and productively instead of choosing the passive-aggressive route. Ending a relationship well requires humility, courage, and mental and emotional discipline.

Here is how to do it:[8]

1. *Focus on your own feelings.* Use "I" language, such as "When you do X, I feel Y" instead of falling into the trap of blaming or accusing the other person. Remember that it is impossible to argue with how you are feeling.

2. *Start with appreciation.* Go back to the beginning of your friendship. Something like, "When we first met, I felt energized spending time together." Chances are you haven't been truthful about what's going on for you, so you might want to apologize for that. "I need to apologize to you for not being honest with you. I have not felt good about spending time together for some time, and I should have said something earlier."

3. *Share exactly how you feel.* For example, "Now when we spend time together, I feel drained and not like I can be really myself."

4. *State what you would be comfortable with.* This part of the conversation goes something like "I no longer want to see you every weekend / spend vacations together. Would you be open to us still meeting a couple of times a year?" If you don't want to meet your friend in the future, don't offer it. Stand firm.

## NOW Leadership... NOW!
### *How to End a Toxic Relationship*

Identify one relationship in your life that is ready to be discontinued. Use the four steps, and jot down your talking points for how to end it. Commit to having the ending talk within the next two weeks.

1. My feeling ("I" language): _____
2. Express appreciation: _____
3. How I feel now: _____

4. What I would be comfortable with: _____
5. I will have this conversation by: _____

## No Deathbed Regrets

In her excellent book *The Top Five Regrets of the Dying: A Life Transformed by the Dearly Departing*, Australian hospice nurse Bronnie Ware interviewed people in hospice care about the regrets they had about their lives. One of the top five regrets is "I wish I'd had the courage to live a life true to myself, not the life others expected of me."[9]

Many (long, we certainly hope) years from now when you are on your deathbed, it's possible you will have some regrets. But I guarantee you that having the humility to admit that you cannot—and should not—try to "do it all" in your life and business will not be one of them. At the end of your life, make sure you feel pleased that you had the humility to eliminate nonessential activities and relationships so you retained time and energy for what truly gave you joy, meaning, and satisfaction.

Leading with Radical Humility means knowing it is impossible to have it all or take part in every option that comes your way. You must ruthlessly make hard trade-offs and get comfortable saying no. Remember, if you don't set your own priorities, somebody else will.

# CHAPTER 5
# FAIL SUCCESSFULLY

*Strength comes not from winning easy battles*
*but from losing hard-fought ones.*
—**Unknown**

## How Do You Embrace Failure for Personal Growth?

For the ten months leading up to June 2005, I was focused on completing one of my lifelong athletic dreams: to finish the solo Race Across America (RAAM), a nonstop three-thousand-mile transcontinental bike race. The gun goes off each year in San Diego, and the clock doesn't stop until the racers arrive in Atlantic City on the East Coast.

Three years earlier, I finished the race with three of my Swiss cross-country skiing buddies in a relay team that took second place. In 2005, I wanted nothing more than to complete it by myself.

To finish, one must average 250 miles every day for twelve straight days and climb well over 170,000 feet. To be competitive, racers stay on the bike for an average of twenty-two out of every twenty-four hours. RAAM is arguably the hardest race on the planet. The only person who has both finished (and won) RAAM and climbed Mount Everest is the Austrian Wolfgang Fasching. He assessed RAAM as significantly more difficult than Everest, both mentally and physically.

In preparation for RAAM, I put my business on hold and significantly reduced all distractions so I could concentrate on my mental and physical training as well as the extensive logistical preparation. RAAM is more like a high-level mountaineering expedition than a typical race. I had a crew of ten people in two vehicles who gave up two-plus weeks of their summer for me. In the months leading up to the race, I was living and breathing RAAM. Not a minute of the day went by without me thinking about some aspect of it and preparing to achieve my goal.

On June 19, 2005, the gun finally went off, and long months of preparation were finally behind me. I purposefully started very slow and clocked in dead last at the first time station (something I am sheepishly still proud about) before descending into the blistering Mojave Desert.

In 110-plus-degree heat, riders started to drop like flies, and I slowly started to cruise through the field. Even RAAM legend Rob Kish, who finished the race an unbelievable seventeen years in succession without a single did-not-finish (DNF) and won it three times, was puking from his bike when I rode past him. The first night brought a welcome cooling of the extreme temperatures. The second and third days came and went, and I continued to feel strong as we started to climb out of Arizona and into Colorado.

But after the third night and into the fourth morning, having ridden almost 850 miles, I found myself on the Colorado Plateau gasping for air and unable to tackle even the smallest hill. That entire morning, I had been coughing white foam, and my vision was getting progressively blurrier as the day wore on.

Riders passed me, and I was unable to even think about hanging with them. Even though I agreed to be interviewed when TV cameras appeared, I knew I was in trouble.

"Seattle's Urs Koenig was not having a good time of it," the broadcaster told the audience. "Struck down by an upper respiratory infection, Koenig was hurting in the high mountain air. The Swiss-born rider crawled up the small climbs, his support car right behind, urging him on. If there is such a thing as the death throes of a RAAM dream, this was it.

"Koenig put on a brave face, sparing time out from his internal struggle to answer a few questions about his race. But his speed was low, his pedaling labored, and it seemed impossible that this man could ride another 2,100 miles in such a condition. But right up until the moment of his withdrawal, Koenig was resolutely positive about the RAAM experience. 'Overall, it's been good,' said Koenig. 'I hope I can get my breathing under control, and I'll be fine.'"

Shortly after the TV crew left and after yet another thirty painful minutes of barely getting anywhere, I decided that I needed to seek medical advice to learn what was going on. My loyal crew loaded the bike in the van, and I crawled in. The following twenty minutes would have been comical if it hadn't been so serious.

Crew member Bruno drove like a maniac toward the next town, Pagosa Springs, Colorado, while crew member Shannon hung out the car window to keep the satellite phone pointed at the sky to call 911—the only means we had to get in touch with the closest medical facility. My bike mechanic, Waz, was trying to keep me from passing out by shaking me violently.

We arrived at the medical facility in Pagosa Springs, where the mood of the friendly, competent staff dramatically changed from laid-back interest to alarm when they discovered that my oxygen saturation was at 42 percent (95–100 percent is normal). I was immediately hooked up to several IVs and given supplemental oxygen. At this point, I still believed I could eventually continue the race and was eagerly asking the attending physician when I could get back on the bike. He quickly talked me out of it when an X-ray revealed fluid had filled my lungs.

Photos from the emergency room also showed me looking puffy. I had put on about six pounds. As it turned out, this was water that was accumulating all over my body. The doctors informed me that I was suffering from severe pulmonary edema—that's the condition people die from on Everest. They said I was lucky to still be alive.

Now it finally all made sense. No wonder I had been laboring for the last fourteen hours and my breathing sounded like a bubble bath (literally!). I was riding at less than 50 percent of my oxygen capacity while my lungs slowly filled with fluid. So instead of riding my bike out of Colorado into Kansas, I took an unfortunate detour and was airlifted to the closest intensive care unit bed in Albuquerque, New Mexico.

I felt devastated. One of my life dreams had just come crashing down. I had invested a full year of training and preparation and put out significant funds. Ending up in the ICU was not part of the game plan. Most of all, I felt that I had let down my crew and all the people who supported me. I felt like an absolute failure. As I was lying in the ICU, I cried and felt utterly hopeless.

Just four days after starting the race full of hope and optimism in San Diego, my dream came to a screeching halt. Five days after that, our epic journey ended when we arrived back home in Seattle. I had failed . . . big-time.

Before I get to the strategies I used to help me fail successfully and come back stronger—strategies that you, too, can implement—I want to point out a few things:

- Know that real failure is to never put yourself in position to fail. Failing and making mistakes are necessary steps in reaching excellence. Only by taking risks will we improve.

- Failure, disappointment, and loss are inevitable parts of our lives and careers. We all understand that intellectually, but it does not make them less painful. Failing is an emotional process, and it can be incredibly tough. Let's not kid ourselves.

- Working through and learning from our failures requires time and energy. On a team level, we must build adequate time and resources into project cycles to identify what is going wrong or what went wrong and what we can learn from it. I will cover the value of an after-action review (AAR) numerous times throughout the book. On a personal level, too, we must create time and space to work through, accept, and learn from our failures.

- A quick note on the word *failure*. I don't buy into feel-good BS that we shouldn't call our mishaps what they are—failures—to somehow make us feel better. Let's call it what it is: I went all in, I gave it my all, and I failed. As a humble leader, you don't need sugarcoating. You accept failure for what it is, work through it by applying the strategies I will outline in this chapter, and come back stronger.

- In chapter 4, I told you how focusing like an elite athlete is important to success because you decrease distractions that get in the way of your goal. That is best practice, but it still doesn't guarantee you'll reach all your goals. Take it from me—a highly motivated, prepared, fit, focused athlete who didn't reach my prized goal in 2005.

As a humble leader, you learn how to fail successfully and model it for your people. Be it a traumatic event like a life-threatening illness, the closing of your business, or simply a career setback or the loss of a major client, you understand the emotional and intellectual road you need to travel to come back stronger. Most of all, you must not be afraid to vulnerably share your setbacks and learnings with your people.

Here are the four research-backed strategies that helped me overcome my RAAM failure. They can help you turn losses into lessons that become building blocks for success.

1. Give emotions of grief time and space.
2. Build mental toughness: apply the ABCD model.
3. Increase resilience. Shift from cause- to response-oriented thinking.
4. Put yourself out there again.

## Give Grief Time and Space

Within two days of my DNF, the voices in my head told me, "Get over it. Come on, it's not that bad. That's just the way it goes sometimes. It's just a bike race. It could have been so much worse," etc., etc. Maybe those voices were speaking the truth. Absolutely, I should have been grateful to be alive. But in those early hours after I had to withdraw, these were all unhelpful thoughts.

To really process your loss, you need to give your strong emotions of disappointment and grief the time and space they deserve. I am not advocating for dwelling on your feelings of loss—you'll see that in the rest of this section. But you do need to really experience these raw emotions. Suppressing them will eventually hinder your ability to learn from your failure. If you do not work through them and process them, they will surface in the most inopportune moments.

Only by allowing the pain, the tears, and the screams of disappointment to show up are you able to really live and work through grief. There is no shortcut there.

While the emotional turmoil of my loss was ongoing, I found it useful to work through the simple ABCD model that the US Army teaches soldiers to increase mental toughness.[1]

## Build Emotional Toughness: Apply the ABCD Model

After Adversity (failure) hits, you experience strong emotions and often shattered Beliefs about yourself and your future. Just like I did. This is a normal response, and the simple ABCD model explicitly calls this out. This in itself is valuable.

- **A.** Adversity
- **B.** Beliefs
- **C.** Emotional Consequences
- **D.** Dispel unrealistic beliefs

In my case, I believed I was a failure because a full year of preparation felt as if it was for naught. I told myself I had disappointed everyone around me. I was devastated. I had so identified with finishing the race that my self-worth was tied to that outcome. I had become so closely attached to the race that when the race went, so did I.

Through sharing and talking through these strong emotional Consequences, feelings, and Beliefs with close friends, my crew, and my family, I was slowly able to accept the loss and see it for what it was: a race that I did not finish. Nothing more, nothing less.

The sharing was hugely valuable. We know that bottling up strong emotions can lead to serious physical and mental symptoms. Further, by talking through my emotion and beliefs and doing my share of self-reflection, I was able to Dispel and reframe the destructive beliefs I was having.

I was able to create a new narrative in which I saw the DNF as a stepping stone in my ultracycling career. It was a very painful experience, yes, but a hugely beneficial one in terms of my own learning. For example, I was better educated about how I needed to fuel during ultraraces, including bringing a crew doctor on board earlier to get hydration right. In short, I was able to Dispel the unrealistic belief that it was all for nothing, that my whole world was coming to an end, and that everyone was disappointed with me.

Here's how I processed my RAAM DNF through the ABCD model:

A. Adversity: I did not finish the RAAM, and I ended up in ICU with a near-death experience.

B. Beliefs: I let everyone down.

C. Emotional Consequences: I am worthless. I am a huge failure.

D. Dispel unrealistic beliefs: I am experiencing a huge disappointment, but I am not the race. I am a worthy athlete and person, DNF or not. This hard experience is an important learning stepping stone in my ultracycling career.

My new narrative also specified the strengths I had to call upon, like my relentless focus to stay on the bike no matter what. I also saw how the experience helped me deepen relationships with some of my crew members. For example, I did not know one crew member, Ken Barnes, particularly well before the race. After RAAM, he became a coaching client for a while, was my crew captain for the next few years, and remains a dear friend to this day.

## Increase Resilience:
## Shift from Cause- to Response-Oriented Thinking

You can increase your resilience by training yourself in how to think about your failure. Instead of focusing on cause-oriented thinking, move quickly to response-oriented thinking.

It is often our reflex to look backward (cause-oriented thinking) from traumatic events to explain what just happened. Such analysis is useful—but only up to a point where strong negative emotions pull you into a downward spiral and prevent you from moving forward. Looking ahead and moving forward showcase response-oriented thinking (table 5.1).

Just to be clear, yes, you need to examine your situation with a ruthless eye and analyze what went wrong. I, for example, critically examined, among many other things, my nutrition logs, which revealed I was overloading with sodium, which was the main contributing factor (and not the altitude as initially suspected) to my pulmonary edema.

This surprising fact was even worth a 2007 academic paper in the journal *Medicine and Science in Sports and Exercise* titled "An Ultracyclist with Pulmonary Edema during the Bicycle Race Across America."[2]

As I stated before: Why do you look back?

To learn.

But when you start to dwell on your feelings of failure and they get in the way of looking ahead, you need to shift from what happened to what is the best course of action given the new realities.

You can build a higher level of resilience in yourself and your team by taking charge of how you think about adversity and moving quickly from analysis to a forward-looking plan of action.

*Table 5.1: Shift from Cause- to Response-Oriented Thinking[3]*

| Cause-Oriented Thinking | Response-Oriented Thinking |
|---|---|
| Was this inevitable, or could I have prevented it? | What part of the situation can I improve? |
| Did I cause it? Or was the cause external? | What positive impact can I have on what happens next? |
| Is the cause specific or widespread? | How can I contain the negatives of the situation and generate currently unseen positives? |
| Is the cause enduring or temporary? | What can I do to address the problem now? |

For me, response-oriented thinking first and foremost meant showing up well with the people who were most important to me at that moment: my crew. I chose to express my deep appreciation for their work and listen to their thoughts and feelings about what to do next.

I did not want to dwell in self-pity or, worse, accuse them of having done something wrong. I have observed these things firsthand in interactions between racers and crew members in extreme situations during ultras when everyone is short on sleep and patience and the pressure is on. Showing up well with my crew was the one thing I knew I could do at that moment to make a positive impact. It was the one thing I could do immediately to improve the situation.

Upon my return to Seattle, I also started right away to reach out to high-altitude medical experts, who helped me get to the bottom of the problem both in the short term and for many years of racing still to come. The question I came to them with was, How could I prevent this from ever happening again? Through many sophisticated medical stress tests, we were able to rule out any underlying condition.

They helped me devise a much better nutrition regime, provided useful input on how to deal with altitude (even though this was only one minor contributing factor to my condition), and made the simple suggestion of weighing myself every six hours during ultraraces. The idea was to be able to immediately detect any potential weight gain due to water retention. A quality scale became part of my ultracycling gear from that day forward.

Looking at what you can do right here, right now, to make things better increases your resilience. Even though it might not feel like you can improve much after a huge letdown, simply being intentional about how you show up with those around you can make a positive impact. Response-oriented thinking puts you back in the driver's seat instead of feeling like a victim.

When my older son, Luc, was ten years old, he broke the growth plate in his ankle while jumping on the trampoline in our backyard with his brother and friends. He had to wear an over-the-knee cast for eight weeks with zero weight-bearing allowed—a challenge for anybody, let alone a spirited young boy. Within a few days of the accident, my resilient ten-year-old created a list. The title was "Things I can still do." It read as follows:

- Play Legos
- Watch Star Wars
- Make a puzzle
- Draw
- Play the claw machine
- Bake chocolate chip cookies

Dad is proud to report that Luc listing out things he could still do versus dwelling on the things he could not do anymore is the perfect embodiment of a response-oriented thinking approach.

# NOW Leadership... NOW!

## *Reflecting on Failure*

Look back over your life and career and identify one failure. Reflect on how that failure made you *feel* at the time, what you *learned* from your experience, and what *positive outcomes* have resulted from that failure.

Bonus: share these three points with an important person in your personal life and/or with your team.

My failure: _____

1. How it made me feel: _____

2. What I learned from the experience: _____

3. What positive outcomes have resulted from my failure: _____

## Putting Yourself Out There Again by Applying Your Growth Mindset

After you have given your emotions of loss time and space, dispelled your unrealistic beliefs about your failure, and focused on response-oriented thinking, it's time to apply your growth mindset and put yourself out there again.

For some, that is easier said than done. We all know people who, after they experience a loss, simply don't. This happens a lot in relationships. The heartbroken person doesn't commit out of fear of getting hurt. Yet here is what I know to be true: The very fact that you've been OK going through a hard loss proves you can do it again if you need to. It's the difference between a fixed mindset and a growth mindset.

In her 2006 book *Mindset: The New Psychology of Success*,[4] Stanford professor Carol Dweck distinguishes two mindsets people tend to have about their basic qualities.

Individuals who believe their talents can be developed through hard work, smart strategies, and input from others have a growth mindset. People with a fixed mindset believe their talents are innate gifts and cannot be improved much. People with a growth mindset tend to achieve more than those with a more fixed mindset, and it's not hard to see why. Those with a growth mindset worry less about looking smart and put more energy into learning.

If you are stuck in a fixed mindset, you will avoid putting yourself out there again because you think your success depends upon protecting and promoting your set of fixed qualities and concealing your deficiencies. Applying a growth mindset, on the other hand, will help you see challenges (and failures) as learning and development opportunities.

My favorite quote by Michael Jordan beautifully sums up the importance of applying a growth mindset and embracing failure and putting yourself out there again: "I've missed more than 9,000 shots in my career. I've lost almost 300 games. Twenty-six times I've been trusted to take the game-winning shot and missed. I've failed over and over and over again in my life. And that is why I succeed."[5] Jordan clearly embraced failing as an integral part of the road to success.

While Jordan most certainly is not the poster child for humility, the lesson still stands: As a humble leader, you understand that failure is a natural byproduct of growth and learning. You embrace failing successfully and model it for your people. Table 5.2 summarizes the Dos and Don'ts of Failing Successfully.

*Table 5.2: Dos and Don'ts of Failing Successfully*

| DO | DON'T |
| --- | --- |
| Make time and space to learn from your failures | Avoid confronting your failures |
| Acknowledge that it is emotionally hard to fail | Put on a false brave face |
| Call it as it is | Sugarcoat |

| DO | DON'T |
| --- | --- |
| Express emotions of loss | Suppress emotions of loss |
| Embrace failure as part of learning and growing | Hide your failures or play it too safely |
| Model failing successfully for your people | Keep your failures close to your vest |
| Identify and dispel unrealistic beliefs | "Become" your unrealistic beliefs |
| Think response oriented | Think cause oriented |
| Embrace a growth mindset | Embrace a fixed mindset |
| Put yourself out there again | Hedge |

## Why I Take an Improv Class

I am currently taking an improv class. Why? It's a highly useful skill to practice as a keynote speaker, and learning a new skill is an excellent way to practice taking risks and failing on a small scale. Improv therefore checks a lot of boxes and also happens to be fun (when it's not terrifying!). Become a lifelong learner by committing to learning one new skill at a time, one after another, professionally or personally.

Here are some of the skills I have been learning over the last few years: meditation, paragliding, nonfiction writing, sailing, speechwriting, avalanche safety, leveraging social media for thought leaders, and kite surfing. What are yours?

## NOW Leadership ... NOW
### Learning a New Skill

Skill I want to learn/improve on: _____

How I am going to do it: _____

## Coming Back Stronger: The Rest of My RAAM Story

Not long after my RAAM DNF, I began applying the new knowledge I was gaining, and soon I was ready to put myself to the test again and compete at a high level. A year after my near-death experience, I had just completed my most successful ultracycling season with a win in the very hilly Ring of Fire twenty-four-hour race by covering 419 miles. I had already won and set a course record (just under fifty-one hours) in a 750-mile race around Washington state and won and set another course record in the 508-mile Race Across Oregon as part of a two-man team.

Sometimes success doesn't look exactly like you thought it would. I never competed in the RAAM again, but I'm sure humbled by the lessons I learned and am proud of how I came back stronger.

I am not sharing this to boast. Plenty of other ultracyclists are far more accomplished than I am. I'm telling you the rest of my story to demonstrate that I was able to overcome the biggest athletic disappointment of my life and follow it up with my best season by applying four very simple strategies. If I can do that, so can you.

# RADICAL HUMILITY
## (THEN) to (NOW)

| What Radical Humility Is Not (THEN) | What Radical Humility Is (NOW) |
| --- | --- |
| Insecure | Confident |
| Indifferent | Ambitious |
| Wavering | Decisive |
| Hero leader: I know | Learning leader: good at not knowing |
| Individual wins | Team wins |
| I tell | I ask |
| Inflated ego | Accurate view of myself |
| Self-promote | Self-reflect |
| Leadership development is touchy-feely | Leadership is a contact sport |
| I listen to tell | I listen to learn |
| Try to do it all | Focus |
| It's all important | Only a few things really matter |
| Rushed ignorance | Thoughtful deliberation |
| Avoid taking risks | Embrace failure as learning |
| Dwell on failures | Look ahead |
| Fixed mindset | Growth mindset |

Scan the QR code below for materials that will help you integrate Shift I: Dig Deep into your daily life:

- reprintable figures
- reprintable tables
- all NOW Leadership . . . NOW prompts from Shift I consolidated in one place
- bonus content—research, quotes, tool kits, and exercises that will help you dig deep

## DIMENSIONS

| | |
|---|---|
| **Self-Knowledge/ Growth Mindset** | **SHIFT I**<br>**DIG DEEP** |
| **Leading Relationally (Team)/ Growth Mindset** | **SHIFT II**<br>**TOUGH ON RESULTS, TENDER ON PEOPLE** |
| | **SHIFT III**<br>**LEAD LIKE A COMPASS** |
| | **SHIFT IV**<br>**FULL TRANSPARENCY** |
| **Leading Relationally (Org.)/ Growth Mindset** | **SHIFT V**<br>**CHAMPION A FEARLESS CULTURE** |

|  THEN  |  | NOW  |
| --- | --- | --- |
| Blind spot | | Self-awareness |
| Trying to do it all | → | Laser-sharp focus |
| Personal failure as a loss | | Failing successfully |
| Transactional relationships at work | | Strong personal relationships at work |
| Feedback that tears down | → | Feedback that builds up |
| Micromanagement | | Front-line empowerment |
| Talent shortage | → | Talent magnet |
| False hero, knows-it-all façade | | Trust through vulnerability |
| Avoidance, secrecy | → | Openness, honesty |
| Afraid to speak up; hide, cover up mistakes | | Psychological safety |
| Fear-driven culture | → | Fearless culture |

**HUMBLE LEADERSHIP = NOW LEADERSHIP**

# SHIFT II
# TOUGH ON RESULTS, TENDER ON PEOPLE

## Humbly Asking the Big Questions:

1. Why is building strong relationships at work your most important task?
2. How do you deliver feedback that builds up versus tears down?

"Tough on results, tender on people" is simple to say but can be difficult to pull off. It requires holding your people to the highest standards while building meaningful and trusting relationships with them.

We have all had bosses who bark orders without regard to the team's well-being and who treat positive morale as office roadkill. They are tough on people. When they are also tough on results, they likely do achieve some strong production for a while but at a steep cost. They breed a culture of fear and intimidation. This is the Fear Zone in the bottom right quadrant of figure II.1. People are afraid to speak up and either hide bad news or only very selectively share it.

When leaders are tough on people and soft on results, they create a culture of indifference (see the bottom left quadrant in figure II.1). The boss might yell at you, but there are no consequences for delivering subpar work, so people simply check out.

On the other hand, when bosses are tender on people and soft on results (top left quadrant), they avoid all conflict. Nothing ever gets corrected. Standards slide. These leaders create a culture of avoidance. Everyone is nice enough toward one another, but the quality of work plummets.

Being tough on results and tender on people means having both high standards and high-touch. It is the ultimate yin-yang of humble leadership, and it's where stellar performance happens (top right quadrant). Tough on results and tender on people requires delivering tough feedback in a human way and caring about your colleagues and direct reports as whole people and not just as worker bees who complete tasks for you.

In this Shift, you will learn (1) why giving a damn about others by building meaningful relationships in your organization is not only the right thing to do by your people but also a business imperative. You will master how meaningful relationships at work lead to better outcomes during a crisis, improve employee engagement, help tear down silos, and make your team more agile, all resulting in better bottom-line results.

You will also learn (2) how to deliver tough feedback that builds up instead of tears down, because direct feedback that is honest and loving is the pathway to elevating performance.

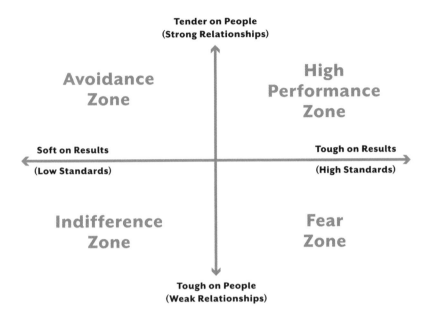

Figure II.1: How Performance Relates
to Tough on Results, Tender on People

# CHAPTER 6
# GIVE A DAMN
# ABOUT OTHERS

*Ubuntu = I am because we are.*
—A concept in Zulu and several other African languages
meaning that a person is a person through other people

## Why Is Building Strong Relationships
## at Work Your Most Important Task?

My Swiss national contingent commander of the NATO peacekeeping
mission in Kosovo, Colonel Franz Gander, was just about to retire to his
modest room in the barracks for the night when his worst nightmare came
true. The following message came via cell phone:

"PLUTO, PLUTO, PLUTO. This is not an exercise. REAL,
REAL, REAL."

The colonel immediately threw his uniform back on and asked his military
assistant to order his staff to the Tactical Operation Center (TOC). Nobody
knew what had happened; they only knew it was bad. PLUTO was known
throughout the contingent as the code name for the worst-case scenario:
one or several members of the unit were either in life-threatening condition
or already deceased. Within minutes the colonel had his staff present. His
chief of staff pulled up orders and procedures for PLUTO.

The staff had been drilled on PLUTO during training, and everybody had
hoped it would always remain just that: an exercise. Instead, the atmosphere

was quiet, tense, and subdued. As the staff got situated, information began to trickle in via cell phones and radio. A Swiss military nurse communicated that a member of the team had suffered a serious heart attack.

The nurse was with the patient, who was being held in critical condition in the military hospital at the base. The attending doctors were all in agreement that he needed immediate open-heart surgery but communicated they were not equipped to perform it there. Time was of the essence, and the doctors on the base recommended a civilian hospital the colonel had never heard of in Pristina, the capital of Kosovo.

The colonel had visited numerous hospitals in Kosovo and knew them to consistently be in dismal condition. Patients often had to purchase and bring their own supplies (scalpels, oxygen, wound care supplies, the whole bit) and then bribe the doctor to perform the surgery. This hospital, however, was different, the military doctors assured him, as it catered specifically to the small corrupt elite in Kosovo plus the sizable expatriate community.

The alternative was to try to transfer the patient back to Switzerland with an air ambulance to get the surgery done back home. However, this would take time that the patient most likely did not have.

How would you decide if this were one of your team members? A timely surgery in a local hospital you are not familiar with or a lengthy transfer back home, which your team member might not survive?

Days later, reflecting on how he and his staff worked through the decision, the colonel shared his lessons with me. The most important one? A well-known motto in the Swiss armed forces and among many crisis management teams: "In Krisen, Köpfe kennen," the colonel said.

Literally translated: "In crises, know the heads."

It pays to build relationships with people before crises occur so you *know* them and can rely on them when a crisis hits. The colonel explained:

> First, it was invaluable to have our nurse present with the patient, updating us on his condition regularly. It was helpful to get to hear from people whom we knew and trusted instead of from the military hospital doctors, whom we did not know.

As we got updates about the patient, my staff and I started immediately to plan for two courses of action in parallel. First, surgery locally. I called the Swiss ambassador to Kosovo, whom I had gotten to know well through our regular meetings, at 11 p.m. and asked her to help me with our due diligence on the local hospital. The ambassador knew the hospital well and assured me that with the right surgeon, it would go as well as back home (she had a colleague in the diplomatic corps who also had emergency surgery there). The ambassador then immediately jumped into action and called a friend who knew the best heart surgeon in Kosovo, and he started to assemble his surgery team immediately.

Second, I called my command in Switzerland and had them put an air ambulance on high alert. The only jet available was the jet for the executive branch of the Swiss government. Because of the strong relationship between our military command and the department of defense, this seemed doable. I had also had coffee with the Italian contingent commander the previous week and happened to know that they had a plane on the ground in Kosovo, so I called him and asked about being able to use their plane if all else failed. He cut through some red tape and put the plane on high alert for us. All this happened between 11 p.m. and 2 a.m. The fact that I could call on several people whom I had built relationships with beforehand proved invaluable. In Krisen, Köpfe kennen!

Fortunately, PLUTO ended well. The patient ended up having surgery in Kosovo, which went splendidly. And after an initial brief recovery phase, the patient was transferred to Switzerland days later, where he made a full recovery.

"In Krisen, Köpfe kennen" is a well-accepted principle in crisis management because when speed is of the essence, strong preexisting relationships—or having given a damn about others—are often more important than detailed reporting guidelines, flowcharts, and orders.

## Be a Mensch . . . for Your People and Performance

Building relationships doesn't just pay off in a crisis. It is also imperative for how you run your teams day to day. Studies on employee engagement consistently show that your people are most engaged when they feel their work matters and you as their boss and their coworkers care for them on a personal level. For example, more than half of the five thousand global respondents to a Glassdoor survey stated that a strong company culture based on trusting relationships is more important to them than salary. A strong relationship culture is even more important to millennials and Generation Z. More than two-thirds of these young adults value culture over money.[1] Further, according to a recent *Great Place to Work* survey, employees who are proud of their work and feel their output matters are twenty times more likely to say theirs is a great place to work.[2]

By now it should be clear that you do not build relationships because you want to be nice or liked. To be sure, it is the right thing to do by your people. Your business reasons are to foster proactive, open communication and to deepen trust, commitment, and engagement throughout the organization. Strong connections within and across your teams help to avoid tribalism and silos that lead to indifference or, worse, manipulation.

I often hear pushback against this suggestion. "I really don't have time for this" is a common response. And I agree. Building and strengthening relationships is often not efficient in the short run because of the time it requires, but when you look at the long-term performance of your team, it always proves more than worth the investment.

Why? First, as the opening story of this chapter about the patient in Kosovo demonstrates, building strong relationships is a powerful tool to deal effectively with complex and ambiguous situations where speed is of the essence.

Second, think about how much drama, distrust, and disengagement you have in your organization. How much does that cost you in dollars and emotional energy—yours and others? You have a choice. You can either build strong collaborative relationships with your people up front, or you can waste time and energy battling unproductive behavior and disengagement at the back end.

Building bonds with others is therefore a preemptive move.

## The Value of Deepening Relationships across Continents and Cultures

My colleague and former Africa program director for Landesa, a US-based land rights NGO, Jennifer Duncan, stresses the importance of preemptively building relationships when she leads teams across continents and cultures.

"Nothing beats spending time together with sleeves rolled up, working, eating, talking, learning about each other, especially when working across continents and cultures," Jennifer told me. "When I was overseeing our work in Tanzania, it took a lot of organizational resources for me to spend time with the Tanzania country office team in Dar es Salaam helping to develop the country's strategic plan. But sharing that time in-country working together and really getting to know one another created a level of familiarity and trust that paid off in spades over the next six to twelve months, when I was mostly in the US and they were mostly implementing projects in Tanzania."

Building and deepening relationships up front ensured that Jennifer and her team could produce outstanding work with little room for misunderstandings and zero drama, even when she, as the manager, was thousands of miles removed from her team for months on end.

"I often reflect on how important those personal relationships were in fostering trust, solidarity, and smart decision-making in an international, intercultural work environment that can be prone to misunderstanding and distrust," she said.

## NOW Leadership ... NOW!
### *Relationship Building Starts with a Conversation*

To develop and deepen relationships, challenge yourself to ask questions that are a bit more personal and share something of yourself that is more personal than you would normally do (within the realm of what is culturally and ethically appropriate, of course). The ideal conversation has you both asking and sharing. There is no magic formula here, and you will need to follow your gut and intuition as the conversation evolves.

Use this list:[3]

**When asking questions:**

- Start asking questions that are culturally acceptable to ask. Life history and personal story are excellent ways to start.
  - Where are you from?
  - How did you get here?

- Listen to responses that are personal, specific, and unique.
- Respond with curiosity and interest. Follow up with more specific questions such as:
  - What do you enjoy most about your work?
  - What are your biggest challenges?
  - How can I/my team best support your work?

**When sharing about yourself with the other person:**

- Share something personal.
- Observe whether the other person seems interested.
- Reveal more or switch to question mode.

The person whom I am going to ask questions that are a bit more personal and share something of myself that is more personal than I normally would is _____

## Relationship Building with a Checklist

In their book *Humble Leadership: The Power of Relationships, Openness, and Trust*,[4] Peter Schein and Edgar Schein share a simple but powerful story about how to build relationships quickly under time pressure and in a highly rigid environment.

David is a senior spine surgeon at a children's hospital. The complex operations of surgery require him to depend deeply on the team he assembles. When asked how he developed a level of trust and openness with his team members, he said he first selected people on their level of competence, and then . . . he took them to lunch.

Why? He realized that the quickest way to reduce hierarchical distance in the team was to do something very human and nonhierarchical together.

Unfortunately, hospital policy changed, and he could no longer have a dedicated team of consistent personnel on a regular basis. He still needed to build trust as quickly as possible, only now he had to do it with rotating strangers.

He evolved the required presurgery checklist into a cooperative process. Instead of hurrying through it, he asked his chief nurse in the operating room to go through each item slowly. Meanwhile, David looked at each team member directly with body language that showed his interest and readiness to hear questions or concerns about each item from each person.

David the spine surgeon displayed humble leadership by utilizing the existing structure of a presurgery checklist. He built and deepened trust by making it a more cooperative process.

Going through the checklist in a respectful, collaborative way created better cohesion and made it safe for David's surgery team members to speak up and ask questions (I will cover the importance of psychological safety in Shift V). Any problems David or other individuals might have missed were caught by the collective, benefiting the team and creating the most important outcome, the patient's improved well-being.

David did not build relationships to be nice or liked. He did it because he knew it would produce the desired results. An important lesson to take away from this story is that relationships can be built fast when done with intentionality.

Relating to others as a whole person and not just as someone who gets stuff done for you is at the foundation of humble leadership and is a conscious choice you can make. It is a skill you already apply in your personal life every day with your friends and family members. You do it by asking questions, by listening, and by opening up about yourself.

# NOW Leadership ... NOW!

## Draw Your Relationship Map

On a piece of paper, write your name in the center and draw around yourself the names and titles of people who are connected to you. For each person, ask yourself:

- How meaningful and trusting is our relationship? (Score from 1 to 5.)
- How meaningful and trusting should this relationship be?

Identify three people, reach out to them, and set up a thirty-minute one-on-one meeting to get to know each other. Plan how you will ask questions and share about yourself to deepen that relationship.

*Figure 6.1: Your Relationship Map*[5]

## What Are Your Team Members' Passions? Ask

Some of the most common complaints about bosses I have heard over the course of my career are the following:

"He does not even know my spouse's name."

"She does not know I am taking care of an aging parent."

"They don't know I am training for a triathlon."

Perhaps you can add your own example here. Many of us have the misconception that being tender on people means we need to bare our soul or let them cry on our shoulder. That is not the case. Our people are simply looking for signs we know they exist beyond the required work they do for us . . . that they matter and we care.

- What *do* you know about your reports' spouses, children, or aging parents?
- What hobbies and activities do they enjoy?
- What aspirations and plans do they have for the years ahead?

These might seem mundane and simple. But paying attention to their answers and truly retaining a bit of information when you ask them questions can make all the difference.

It really is the little things. We all want to be heard and seen as a whole person and not just as a worker bee.

Our virtual work following the pandemic has made it even more important to be intentional about these "get to know you" conversations. Long gone for many are the days when CEOs and interns could at least share a quick water cooler conversation—and this is a big loss.

One of the things I institutionalize at all the places I work aims at making sure we all get to know one another better on a personal level. I give everybody on the team thirty minutes to share an interest of theirs with the team. I did this in my academic career, with business teams, and during my peacekeeping command. There is only one guideline: you need to be passionate about whatever you are presenting.

During my peacekeeping command, we learned

- what it's like to be a chef in a busy downtown hotel in Bangkok,
- what the life of a professional DJ is like,
- the passion one team member had for her picturesque mountain hometown,
- the work of an airplane mechanic,
- the thrill and excitement of skydiving,
- and much, much more.

Most importantly, though, we got to know one another on a more meaningful level with a deepened appreciation for one another. As a result, trust and cooperation improved within the group.

Getting to know your team members as people helps you apply the "platinum rule of leadership." The Golden Rule states that you treat and motivate others like you want to be treated and motivated. The platinum rule says that you treat and motivate others how *they* want to be treated and how *they* want to be motivated.

## NOW Leadership ... NOW!
### *What Are You Doing This Weekend?*

This coming Friday—yes, this Friday—make a point of asking the team member you know least about their weekend plans. Just one person. And then on Monday, check in with them about how their weekend was. That's it. One team member and their weekend plans.

The person I am going to ask about their weekend plans is _____

## Strong Relationships Make for an Agile Organization

We saw firsthand at the onset of the COVID-19 pandemic that tightly networked organizations were more agile and resilient when within days we all had to move to doing business virtually. My clients who ran or were part of organizations that were founded on meaningful, trusting relationships across departments adapted much more quickly to this new virtual reality than those where folks from different departments rarely communicated with one another.

Some actual examples from my well-networked clients' organizations included the following:

- Need help with setting up your virtual home office? Call the IT person whom you had drinks with at last year's off-site and chatted with about your mutual interest in photography.
- Need support in processing payments 100 percent online? Call the person in finance whom you exchanged notes with about your kid's soccer team coach over coffee last month.
- What is going on with those folks in marketing whom you used to have an excellent rapport with, as they were working just down the hall from you, but now aren't delivering the numbers you need to get your job done? Get in touch with the marketing director you had lunch with to kick off this current project.

Strong relationships make for agile, nimble, and adaptable teams. I would even go a step further. Resilient organizations get stronger when they are tested, much like an immune system. Why? Our relationships strengthen when we go through hard experiences together. When the famous stuff hits the fan, we can work through it as a team.

Of course, some relationships do not survive stressful experiences, but if they do, they almost always come out stronger on the other side. Just think of a difficult time you went through with a dear friend. Likely the experience further cemented your bond. The same goes for teams. When stressed, agile teams do better. Early data and anecdotal evidence have suggested that strong cultures based on meaningful personal relationships before the pandemic tended to become even stronger through the stress of the pandemic, while weak cultures further declined.[6]

You might feel you already blew your shot at connecting with longtime coworkers. The relationships with them, good or bad, are already established, and this relationship building will only work with new employees. My challenge to you is this: there is no time like the present. Every relationship can grow and develop, even long-standing ones. Use the relationship map you just created to assess all your relationships, the old and the new, and start taking proactive steps to (re)build and deepen connections. See table 6.1 for a summary of the business reasons for meaningful relationships at work.

*Table 6.1: Business Reasons for Meaningful Personal Relationships at Work*

| Transactional Relationships at Work | Meaningful Relationships at Work |
| --- | --- |
| In crisis: Slow response by following rules and procedures | In crisis: Ability to move fast by knowing the right people and cut through red tape |
| Disengagement | Engagement |
| Turnover | Retention |
| Secrecy, avoidance | Transparent communication |
| Drama, unproductive behavior | Trust, commitment |
| Takes no time | Can be developed fast with intention |
| Golden rule of leadership | Platinum rule of leadership |
| Show up for the job only, then leave | Bring whole self to work |
| Siloed teams and organizations | Resilient, agile teams and organizations |
| Under stress: Fall apart | Under stress: Get stronger |
| Might be efficient in the (very) short term | Always effective in the long term |

## Beyond "Everyone Else Sucks"

Close your eyes and imagine the best-performing team in your organization. Really visualize how they interact, how they communicate. What is the level of trust? How would you describe their relationships?

I'll bet you any amount of money that your best-performing team operates at an incredibly high level of trust and that team members have strong, meaningful relationships with one another and their boss. You might have asked yourself this magical question we often ask ourselves: Wouldn't it be great if all my teams operated like my best-performing team? But how on earth do I pull this off?

This was exactly the task that now-retired four-star general Stan McChrystal, whom we met at the start of chapter 2, faced in 2003 when he took command of the task force fighting terror in the Middle East.

How could he scale the quality of his best special operations teams—the Army Rangers, Navy SEALs, or Green Berets—across his command of thousands of men and women?

Ironically, many of the traits that make your very best team so great are incredibly difficult to scale across your organization. Outstanding teams often define themselves by not being like "the other guys." Not exactly the most conducive attitude toward collaboration.

As McChrystal reports in his book *Team of Teams: New Rules of Engagement for a Complex World*, "Though any given SEAL was, like the entire task force, on paper fighting the same fight, he was really fighting for his squad . . . The bonds within squads are fundamentally different than those between squads or other units. In the words of one of our SEALs: 'The squad is the point at which everyone else sucks. The other squadron sucks, the other SEAL teams suck, and our army counterparts definitely suck'"[7]

The goal then becomes to accomplish missions better than the team bunking on the other side of the base rather than to win the war.

This is worth stressing: the very things that make great teams outstanding—deep trust, emotional bonds, seamless communication—often make them incompatible with other teams because of the mindset that "everyone else sucks" beyond my team.

This, of course, is reminiscent of the silo mentality prevalent in so many organizations.

McChrystal needed to move his task force beyond the point where everyone else sucked. He needed to scale what made his best teams outstanding.

His solution? Build strong relationships across his task force through a *team of teams* approach in which not everyone needed to have a relationship with everybody else, but everybody needed to know *someone* on every other team.

This is key and important enough to repeat: everyone knows someone on every other team. For example, every salesperson knows *someone* in marketing, *someone* in finance, *someone* in operations, research, HR, and so on. So when your salespeople have to work with these other departments, they think of them as friendly colleagues instead of competing rivals.

As a result of transforming from discrete silos to becoming better-networked, McChrystal's task force became measurably more effective, and its speed and precision improved significantly. Importantly though, as he points out, this was not a triumph of fine-tuning the task force into a hyperefficient machine. It was the result of becoming a more resilient and adaptable organization through systematically developing and deepening relationships at all levels and all communication lines.

As a humble leader, you must make relationship building your top leadership priority. Rather than primarily leaning on content expertise, you need to shift to prioritizing creating the right environment.

## Team of Teams with a Business Purpose at the UN

A few weeks after I deployed to the UN military peacekeeping mission in the Middle East in 2020, I had the honor of getting appointed as Swiss senior national representative (SNR). It was my job to represent the commander of all Swiss peacekeeping operations in the mission. I also was tasked with representing the Swiss officer to both mission leadership as well as to our home command.

In true pragmatic Swiss armed forces fashion, where skills are often more valued than rank, I was appointed SNR even though I was not the highest-ranking Swiss officer in the mission, something no other nation would ever dream of doing (apparently, I had made a decent impression along the way). This made my job harder, though, as I needed to go the extra mile to be taken seriously among the higher-ranked officers.

Making my SNR job even more challenging was the fact that I was deployed to an outstation in Lebanon, far away from mission headquarters in Jerusalem, which, because of COVID-19 travel restrictions, was even more isolated. I knew that to be effective, I needed to establish and grow my relationship network in the mission, and I needed to do it fast!

Immediately after my appointment, I took a page out of McChrystal's playbook. Together with my SNR predecessor and some colleagues who had been in the mission longer than me and knew their way around, I pulled out the mission org chart and started to systematically identify key military and civilian personnel in all departments and outstations as well as SNRs of other large troop-contributing countries. I knew I needed to know at least someone on every team. I also identified all current and soon-to-be-deployed Swiss officers. When done, I had an initial list of approximately thirty people I needed to build relationships with.

Then I got to work. Over the next ten days, I spent most hours I was not patrolling the cease-fire line between Israel and Lebanon on video conferences and calls. For each of my thirty-minute relationship-building meetings, I had the same basic outline:

1. briefly introduce myself,
2. learn as much as I could about the other person's responsibilities and their professional and personal background, and
3. learn their expectations of me as Swiss SNR.

I followed my coaching rule by putting on my listening ears: at least 80 percent listening, no more than 20 percent talking. Without exception (even up to senior mission leadership), folks were appreciative of me making the effort to get to know them. But these relationship-building meetings had a clear business purpose, and the benefits were apparent pretty much immediately. Within weeks of my appointment as SNR, several Swiss officers deployed in our mission in Syria voiced serious safety concerns that they did not feel were taken seriously by their local commander. They asked me for help in my function as SNR.

In large part because I already had made the effort to get to know key mission staff on a personal level and establish a relationship without a business agenda up front, my voice was heard and taken seriously at the highest levels. The concerns of my officers were immediately addressed and resolved.

Relationship building with a business purpose—one of the core elements of humble leadership—had paid off!

# CHAPTER 7
# I LOVE YOU, AND YOUR WORK IS NOT GOOD ENOUGH

*People don't care how much you know
until they know how much you care.*
—**Attributed to Theodore Roosevelt,
John Maxwell, Earl Nightingale, and others**

## How Do You Deliver Feedback That Builds Up Versus Tears Down?

I was out of breath from pushing my bike up the steep hill. My backpack, filled with clothes, a sleeping bag, and camping cookware, was strapped to the back of my bike and felt incredibly heavy. I took a brief rest to catch my breath and scanned the top of the hill.

I was twelve years old and on my way home from a fun but intense and tiring weekend camping in the woods with my Boy Scout troop. My parents were tough. While other kids were picked up in their parents' cars, my mom and dad made it clear: "We support you attending Scouts, but you must be willing to ride your own bike. We are not shuttling you back and forth."

Which is exactly why I was now hauling my bike with my heavy backpack up that damn hill.

My parents loved me; I knew that. They were tender, but they were also tough. Want to join an activity? Go for it. But you figure out how to get to and from there yourself.

Just as I started to walk uphill again, I spotted my dad riding his bike toward me. I was surprised to see him. He slowed down, did a U-turn, and greeted me with his trademark "Mano" (one of his many nicknames for me derived from "man," which I now use with my own boys as well).

"How was it?" he asked. "I thought I would meet you halfway so you don't have to make your way back home by yourself. Would you like me to take your backpack?"

I felt elated to see him and grateful that I did not have to make the long way home by myself (and yes, I was thankful he was offering to carry my heavy backpack). Meeting me on my way home so we could spend some time together was my dad's way of showing me that he loved and cared for me.

As we started to walk up the hill together, both pushing our bikes, he inquired about the activities I enjoyed and about my Scout friends. As a former Scout and avid outdoorsman, he truly cared about my experience and genuinely wanted to know about it. I was excited to tell him everything. He was a caring and understanding listener. This feeling of being truly heard then made it easier for me to hear the hard feedback he had for me a few minutes later: "Mano, you forgot one of the most important items on your packing list at home. Do you know what it is?"

I honestly had no idea. He answered his own question.

"Your emergency first-aid kit. Not good, Urs. Not good. Weak, very weak."

Forgetting your emergency first-aid kit at home might not seem like a big thing to you, but it was for me, and my dad knew it. His highly disciplined military approach of always having the complete gear list (including emergency supplies) for outdoor adventures was deeply ingrained in me. It has served me well during many trips up to this day. Rarely do I forget anything on my various travels.

He rode his bike to accompany me on my way home. He offered to take my heavy backpack. He genuinely asked and cared about my experience. He showed me that he loved me. And *at the same time* he made it abundantly clear that forgetting my first-aid kit was not acceptable and he disapproved: I love you, and your work is not good enough. (You will find my very personal tribute to my dad—one of the best leaders I have ever known—between the two chapters of Shift V.)

## Radical Candor

The notion that feedback is much more likely to be heard and acted upon by your team members if you've built strong relationships with them might seem obvious today. However, this is a very recent phenomenon. The leader-as-hero paradigm I covered in chapter 2, with an all-knowing, sole expert at the top directing and commanding his people—and it almost always was a he—like pawns on a chessboard, has been deeply ingrained in us for many generations.

Connecting with and caring for team members was unnecessary for someone in that position. The leaders knew best and made all the decisions, and if the rank and file disagreed, he simply got rid of those who dared question him and brought someone new in. This is an oversimplification, of course, but the fact stands: relationship building between boss and employees was not a high priority.

This has started to change over the last decade. Former Silicon Valley executive Kim Scott popularized for the mainstream business world the importance of giving direct and honest feedback in her outstanding book *Radical Candor*.[1]

Scott describes the two dimensions crucial to becoming a great boss. The first she calls "caring personally," which is building deep personal relationships with your people, bringing your whole personal self to work, and encouraging the people who work for you to do the same.

Importantly, there is a second dimension, and that is telling people when their work is not up to par. It is delivering hard feedback about the quality of your team members' work and holding them to high standards. Scott calls this dimension "challenging directly."

Of course, directly challenging people you care about can be difficult. Many people struggle with it. But as a leader, you must accept that sometimes people will be angry with you for the decisions you are responsible for making. In fact, I would argue that if they are not, you are not doing enough challenging.

Combining *caring personally* and *challenging directly* is what makes a kick-ass boss. When your people know you care deeply about them, they will be able to hear both your praise and criticism.

Jacqueline Carter and Rasmus Hougaard, in their book *Compassionate Leadership: How to Do Hard Things in a Human Way*,[2] demonstrate with quantitative research how doing hard things courageously *and* in a compassionate way greatly benefits you as a leader. Their data shows when you embody Shift II (tough on results, tender on people), you get promoted faster, reduce your stress, and are half as likely to want to quit your job. Further, it positively impacts your team members. Teams of tough and tender leaders report higher job satisfaction, better engagement, and less burnout. Importantly, they also produce better business results.

Former Secretary of State Colin Powell is another powerful example of a highly ambitious *and* humble leader. His career took him from his Harlem childhood as the son of Jamaican immigrants to top positions in the US military and federal government before ultimately being marred by the misleading speech he gave at the United Nations that justified the Iraq invasion in 2003.

Yet Powell had the humility to own that disastrous misjudgment. Only a few years later, he publicly stated that he had been gravely mistaken. Powell's rise to the top showed his ambition, but he also had the humility to admit when he was wrong.

Powell's "I love you, and your work is not good enough" leadership principles are as follows:[3]

1.  "The day soldiers stop bringing you their problems is the day you have stopped leading them. They have either lost confidence that you can help them or concluded that you do not care. Either case is a failure of leadership."
2.  "Being responsible sometimes means pissing people off."

Aside from the importance of caring for your people, Powell highlights in his first principle an important challenge you must tackle as a leader. In many organizations, asking for help is seen as weakness or failure. Whether it's said in so many words or merely implied, the prevailing principle often is this: don't bring me problems; bring me solutions. As a result, people often cover up their gaps, and results suffer.

Let me be clear. I am not advocating that your people should act helplessly and run to you with every little trouble. But you do need to make yourself accessible and available when you're needed and when you might be able to help your people find a way to overcome an obstacle. You can show genuine concern for their challenges and provide support even as you demand high standards.

# NOW Leadership ... NOW!
## *With or Without You*

Make a list of three problems you expect your people to solve without your input (for example, technical issues in their area of expertise). Now write down a list of three problems you want them to present to you for support (e.g., lack of resources, competing priorities). At your next team meeting, share, discuss, and clarify this list with your team.

Problems my team needs to solve without my input:

1. _____
2. _____
3. _____


Problems my team needs to bring to my attention:

1. _____
2. _____
3. _____

As Powell writes in his second principle, strong leadership means being a responsible adult in the room and taking full ownership of business outcomes. This means some people will get angry at your actions and will disagree with your decisions. It's inevitable when you're the boss. If you make the tough decisions and confront people who need to be held accountable, you will piss some people off, *and* you are doing your job well!

I often joke with my clients that upsetting everyone a little is a sign that you are doing an excellent job as a leader. By procrastinating on difficult choices by trying not to make anyone mad, you're simply ensuring the only people you'll wind up angering are the best producers on your team. Don't fall into that trap.

Sometimes that means firing someone. When individuals break rules, take immoral or dangerous shortcuts, or repeatedly refuse to adhere to agreed-upon norms, letting them go can be the most productive response. As a leader, you are always onstage, and your people are observing your every move. They observe what you do and don't do, what you say and don't say. When a firing is a productive response on your part, your people will notice that you took swift action.

The power of pissing off your people is beautifully displayed in one of my favorite sports movies, *Miracle*, which tells the story of the 1980 US men's Olympic hockey squad, which beat the highly favored Soviet Union juggernaut. Coach Herb Brooks pushes his team so hard that they despise him. He unites his players by giving them a common enemy: him. It also becomes clear, though, that he personally cares about each of his players. Only with time do they start to appreciate and value his approach to coaching.

The moral is this: As a leader you must work on building authentic relationships while also accepting the reality that you are going to be disliked and maybe even hated at times.

# NOW Leadership ... NOW
## *Challenging and Caring*

What is one tough piece of feedback you know you need to give but have procrastinated and not yet given? By when will you do it?

My tough feedback is _____

to _____

by _____


What is one act of being tender on people you have not performed but want to (a compliment, a thank-you note, an act of service, a gift)? By when will you do it?

My tender act is _____

for _____

by _____


## How to Raise Your Voice

When you are tough on results, you must adhere to these two rules of leadership 99 percent of the time:

1. Praise in public; criticize in private.
2. Don't raise your voice. Stay calm and collected.

Knowing how to act in the other 1 percent of situations and learning how to properly raise your voice with your people can make or break you as a great leader. (You'll see how I handled one of my 1 percent of situations in chapter 11.)

I bet you are thinking, *Wait! How do you reconcile raising your voice with being tender on people?*

You might disagree that getting loud is a method to ever pursue NOW. I debated this long and hard. Plenty of colleagues challenged me on it ("Isn't getting loud exactly the old-school THEN leadership that breeds fear and intimidation?"). In principle I agree, but hear me out. I believe there are rare occasions when raising your voice with your team members can be effective to uphold standards. For example, when one of your reports acts like a prima donna and openly disrespects you or one of the team members. Or when a near-and-dear team value is openly being kicked to the curb—even, or perhaps especially, when it comes from an exceptionally talented performer.

I want to emphasize again that raising your voice applies only in very rare situations. Save the strongest words and tone for when they are needed. In the spirit of situational leadership, I believe turning up the volume can have its place as long as it's used extremely sparingly, it's controlled, the words are clear and chosen wisely, and you've already built trust with your team and as a result, your relationship with your team can handle it.

In the hilarious Apple TV show *Ted Lasso*, Coach Lasso stays calm and collected throughout the first five episodes despite experiencing tons of disrespect from . . . well . . . everybody: players, media, the owner, and the fans . . . until he chooses not to stay calm anymore. Lasso's star player, Jamie Tartt, is faking an injury to get out of training, or "practice." This is a red line for the affable coach.

As Lasso is walking out of the locker room to his office, Tartt says, "Relax, Ted. It's just practice."

Lasso slows down and turns around. The locker room goes quiet as players awkwardly move out of the way. Lasso slowly approaches Jamie, who is sitting on the bench. Lasso stands in front of Jamie and starts in a calm voice.

> Hey, you can't practice, you can't practice. You are hurt, you are hurt. It's as simple as that . . . But it ain't about that. It ain't about that at all. You are sitting in here. You are supposed to be the franchise player, and yet here we are talking about you missing practice. Practice, you understand me? [Now he slowly starts to raise his voice] Practice, not a game, not a game, not the game you go out there and die for, right? Play every weekend like it's your last, right? No, we are talking

about practice, man. Practice. You know you are supposed to be out there. You know you are supposed to lead by example. You are just shoving all that aside.

So here we are, Jamie, we are talking about practice. [And now raising his voice] Not a game. Not THE game. We are talking about practice, PRACTICE with your team, with your teammates. The only place that we get to play together, that we've got control over. The rest of the time is us eleven against those eleven. [And now yelling] We are talking about practice, man. I AM TALKING ABOUT PRACTICE, MAN. And you can't do it because you're hurt, right? [And now in a calm voice again] It's fine by me. I tell you what. Do me a favor when you get out there. Set the cones so the other reserves can do a little passing drill.

With respect already established with the rest of his players, Ted lashing out is a clear message to every single team member on the importance of PRACTICE! (The sports fans among you will recognize this scene is a spoof of NBA basketball player Allen Iverson's infamous press conference in 2002.)

Here are the things to remember before you raise your voice:

- Use it sparingly and very consciously. Don't let your emotions run away with you.
- Only use volume because you care . . . not to humiliate or degrade people.
- Raising your voice is not the same thing as swearing or calling people names. Know the difference.

By putting on a bit of a tantrum and publicly laying into someone, you make a public statement about where your line in the sand is. If used with intention and restraint, it can be an incredibly powerful leadership tool. When done well, your voice raising can reconfirm the commitment to the team's values. Remember while you address only one (or a few) people, your audience is the whole team, meaning you are sending a very strong message to everybody.

## Military Unit Strength through Tough Love

I was sitting in my boss's office at HQ during my first week as team commander in Kosovo. The colonel turned to me and said, "I love you, Urs. You know I do, *and* this is not good enough. I know you can do better."

His words made me shrink in my chair . . . mostly because I knew he was right and because I hated nothing more than disappointing him. He was the best commander I ever had. He was the embodiment of *tough on results, tender on people* and I'm sure part of the inspiration for my emphasis on it in my coaching business and my own leadership before I had even identified it as such. He was demanding and settled for nothing less than our best. He pushed when our deliverables weren't up to par, and he beamed when they were. He challenged us when he knew we were capable of more, and that was what he was doing in this moment: "I love you, Urs, *and* this is not good enough."

He offered up praise, appreciation, and thanks when we were at our best. He was a master at combining empathy and accountability . . . and here I was disappointing him with subpar work.

Two nights prior at 0200, I was sitting alone in my office feeling utterly exhausted and hardly able to keep my eyes open. Unfortunately, against my better judgment, I had left the most important task for last: rewriting my team's operational orders, which spelled out everything from how my unit would accomplish our mission to the guiding principles of our working and living together. It was an important document. The deadline was 0700 that morning. I plowed through it, and two hours later, at 0400, I thought I was finally done. I drafted the email to my chief of staff, attached the ops order, and then hit send. I was finally able to get a few hours of shut-eye.

Sitting in my boss's office, I now heard in no uncertain terms what I already knew deep down: in my sleep-deprived state, I had submitted work that was a far cry from my best thinking. Right then and there, I vowed to myself to never disappoint him and myself again. Indeed, I never did. My commander's golden combination of tough on results, tender on people made me stretch myself to the highest standards. For the entire remainder of our mission, everything that I delivered to his desk was double-checked by at least two people. Simply put, unless we felt proud of the product, we would rework it until it was of top-notch quality.

His approach brought out the best in me and all the commander's other direct reports. We in turn saw how it brought out the best in our teams. As a result, our entire unit became infinitely stronger. Consider figure 7.1 your very own "I love you and your work is not good enough" checklist.

*Figure 7.1: I Love You, and Your Work Is Not Good Enough Checklist*

| | |
|---|---|
| ✓ | Do hard things courageously. |
| ✓ | Do hard things in a human way. |
| ✓ | Challenge your people directly. |
| ✓ | Care deeply and personally for your people. |
| ✓ | Piss your people off (sometimes). |
| ✓ | Clarify the sort of issues you expect your people to bring to you. |
| ✓ | Clarify the sorts of challenges you expect your people to solve without your involvement. |
| ✓ | Accept being disliked. |
| ✓ | Know when and how to raise your voice. |

## To Show You That I Am Sure You'll Never, Ever Do This Again . . .

Returning to his home in Los Angeles from an air show in San Diego, test pilot Bob Hoover suddenly had both engines shut off in midflight. Using his experience and some skillful maneuvering, he managed an emergency landing, but the plane was badly damaged. Thankfully, neither Hoover nor his two passengers were hurt.

Hoover's first course of action after the emergency landing was to inspect the airplane's fuel. Just as he suspected, the World War II propeller plane had been fueled with jet fuel instead of gasoline.

Upon returning to the airport, he asked to see the mechanic who had serviced his airplane. The young man was sick with agony over his mistake. Tears streamed down his face as Hoover approached. He had just caused the loss of a very expensive plane and could have caused the loss of three lives as well.

No one would've blamed Hoover for ripping into the mechanic for his carelessness. But Hoover did not. He didn't even scold or criticize the mechanic. Instead, he put his big arm around the man's shoulder, looked at him sternly, and said with a firm voice, "To show you that I'm sure that you'll never, ever do this again, I want you to service my F-51 tomorrow."

As told in Dale Carnegie's classic book *How to Win Friends & Influence People*,[4] by choosing this calm, trusting, empathetic, and very direct way to communicate with the mechanic, Hoover made it safe for the man to own his mistake and make good on it: I love you, and your work is not good enough.

This concept is relevant to leaders at all levels in every industry. It's as simple as having compassion for other people and recognizing the value to them and you when you treat them with respect. Yet it's put to the test when things go sideways. How will you respond when they do?

The notion that you have to be either a nice person or a tough leader is a false dichotomy. As a humble leader, you understand that being a good human and executing what needs to be done are *not* mutually exclusive. We can all courageously do hard things in a human way!

# RADICAL HUMILITY

## (THEN) to (NOW)

| What Radical Humility Is Not (THEN) | What Radical Humility Is (NOW) |
|---|---|
| Insecure | Confident |
| Indifferent | Ambitious |
| Wavering | Decisive |
| Hero leader: I know | Learning leader: good at not knowing |
| Individual wins | Team wins |
| I tell | I ask |
| Inflated ego | Accurate view of myself |
| Self-promote | Self-reflect |
| Leadership development is touchy-feely | Leadership is a contact sport |
| I listen to tell | I listen to learn |
| Try to do it all | Focus |
| It's all important | Only a few things really matter |
| Rushed ignorance | Thoughtful deliberation |
| Avoid taking risks | Embrace failure as learning |
| Dwell on failures | Look ahead |
| Fixed mindset | Growth mindset |

| What Radical Humility Is Not (THEN) | What Radical Humility Is (NOW) |
|---|---|
| Transactional relationships | Giving a damn about your people |
| Human resources | See each team member as a whole person |
| Build relationships to be "nice" | Build relationships with a business purpose |
| Tear others down | Build others up |
| Deliver tough feedback in a tough way | Deliver tough feedback in a humane way |
| Low standards | High standards |

Scan the QR code below for materials that will help you integrate Shift II: Tough on Results, Tender on People into your daily life:

- reprintable figures
- reprintable tables
- all NOW Leadership . . . NOW prompts from Shift II consolidated in one place
- bonus content—research, quotes, tool kits, and exercises that will help you be tough on results, tender on people

## DIMENSIONS

**Self-Knowledge/
Growth Mindset**

## SHIFT I
## DIG DEEP

**Leading
Relationally (Team)/
Growth Mindset**

## SHIFT II
## TOUGH ON RESULTS,
## TENDER ON PEOPLE

## SHIFT III
## LEAD LIKE A COMPASS

## SHIFT IV
## FULL TRANSPARENCY

**Leading
Relationally (Org.)/
Growth Mindset**

## SHIFT V
## CHAMPION A
## FEARLESS CULTURE

|  THEN  |  |  NOW  |
| --- | --- | --- |
| Blind spot | | Self-awareness |
| Trying to do it all |  | Laser-sharp focus |
| Personal failure as a loss | | Failing successfully |
| Transactional relationships at work |  | Strong personal relationships at work |
| Feedback that tears down | | Feedback that builds up |
| Micromanagement |  | Front-line empowerment |
| Talent shortage | | Talent magnet |
| False hero, knows-it-all façade |  | Trust through vulnerability |
| Avoidance, secrecy | | Openness, honesty |
| Afraid to speak up; hide, cover up mistakes | → | Psychological safety |
| Fear-driven culture | | Fearless culture |

**HUMBLE LEADERSHIP = NOW LEADERSHIP**

# SHIFT III
# LEAD LIKE
# A COMPASS

## Humbly Asking the Big Questions:

1. How do you empower your team?
2. How do you become a talent magnet?

Today's hypercompetitive, volatile business climate requires quick action at the front lines. With speed and urgency increasing, our people often do not have time to feed a question up the chain and wait for a response back. Employees who are empowered to make fast decisions independently will drive your success. They have internalized the shared purpose of your team. When faced with a just-in-time decision, they ask themselves, "Will this help us achieve our purpose?"

From employees waiting for directions from the boss (THEN) to empowered employees proactively making smart decisions (NOW), and from micromanagement (THEN) to empowered execution at the front line (NOW), success as a humble leader is measured by how the ship runs when you aren't there.

This requires you to have the humility to let go of control and authority and shift from a controlling "hands-on" (THEN) to a "hands-off" (NOW) approach. It requires you to challenge yourself on every decision you make to ask, Who on my team is in the best position to make this decision? Whom should I delegate decision-making authority to?

In this Shift, you will learn (1) how to master clarity of shared purpose so you can lead like a compass by showing your people true north versus providing them with a detailed map on how to get there. When you lead like a compass, you will become *less involved* but *more relevant* as a leader. And you will learn (2) how to transform your team into a leadership factory.

In the process you will become a talent magnet with employees who have potential lining up wanting to work for you. When you attract and grow the best and brightest, you build capacity to delegate and empower, which frees you to lead like a compass.

# CHAPTER 8
# CLARITY OVER CONTROL

*Our one rule: Use good judgment in all situations.*
**—Nordstrom's one-rule employee handbook**

## How Do You Empower Your Team?

Finally! With a heavy sigh, I plunged myself into my airplane seat in Pristina, Kosovo. I kicked off my combat boots, opened my uniform top, pushed the seat back, and took a deep breath . . . ahh . . .

The doors closed, the engines revved, and the plane rolled down the taxiway. I felt exhausted, relieved, and excited all at the same time. After seven long months, I was finally on my way to see my boys back in Seattle, USA, for a long-awaited leave from my peacekeeping command.

The plane turned onto the runway and came to a complete stop. Then the engines started to roar full throttle. Even after thousands of plane rides, I still love this part. The plane began to slowly move, then accelerate faster, pushing me back in my seat.

As we lifted off the ground, I looked down on the landscape of this troubled nation of Kosovo and reflected on my team, now in the capable hands of my deputy commander.

Not for one minute did I feel nervous about leaving my team alone—not over the last few months when I occasionally had to travel to HQ for a day of meetings, and not now for ten days of leave with my boys back home. I knew my team was set up for success in my absence.

How did we get there?

I did what I have always done in every position I have ever held to ensure my team would work well without me: I empowered my people. There are many strategies to make that happen, but the simplest answer to how I achieve this is that I have them network with and learn from others at all levels and locations.

Let me give you one example from my peacekeeping mission. Our team's daily deliverables were called daily situation reports (DSRs). The DSRs summarized our findings from the previous twenty-four hours and had to be delivered to the staff at HQ at 1700 every day. The recipients of our DSR were staff officers at HQ. I called them our "clients."

I had my team members shadow these staff officers for a day or two. By working alongside them and spending time together, my people gained a thorough understanding and appreciation for the needs and pain points of these staff officers. As a direct result of this increased understanding and appreciation for the needs of our clients, the quality of our DSRs improved significantly.

Just as importantly—maybe more so—by having Turkish coffee after lunch or a drink after work, my team members and these staff officers developed and deepened personal relationships. In turn, collaboration significantly improved between HQ and my teams. Instead of having all communication flow through me as the sole liaison, my team members felt empowered to pick up the phone and call HQ directly to get their questions answered. This removed me as a potential bottleneck.

On a broader level, having my team members get to know others at all levels of the peacekeeping force helped to increase our understanding of the high-level strategic environment we were operating in and—crucially important—empowered them to make smart, independent decisions instead of waiting for my direction.

For months, I had not been a bottleneck. I had not been the sole liaison to HQ. I had not been the sole strategic decision-maker. That is why now, as I rested comfortably on the plane as it climbed through the clouds, I never for one second doubted the ability of my team to do a superb job without me.

## Be Less Involved So You Can Be More Relevant

April 15, 2013, was a glorious spring morning in Boston. Massachusetts governor Deval Patrick had a thing of rare beauty to look forward to, a day without official appointments.

Patrick was driving home after a workout, and as an avid gardener felt elated about the prospect of messing around in the soil that afternoon. That was when his head of emergency management called from the finish line of the Boston Marathon. "Governor, we have an unbelievable disaster here . . . a horrible scene. We need to set up a communication center. We'd like you to come down."

You probably remember how you felt when you first heard the horrific news about the Boston Marathon bombing: disbelief, helplessness, maybe anger. What most of us are less familiar with is the highly effective and collaborative response to the bombing—widely credited as the most effective and collaborative response to a disaster ever studied. One key reason, according to experts who researched the response, was the leadership practiced by

Governor Patrick. Every time he entered the command center, instead of telling people what to do, he would ask, "How can I help?"[1]

The governor's leadership set a tone that spread through all the response teams and agencies. Patrick was keenly aware of the common trap leaders fall in during a crisis: micromanage to feel in control (THEN). They grab the reins and yank them, overstepping into areas best handled by specialists. Instead, he empowered by delegating responsibility and authority to those best suited for the job (NOW).

Patrick chose to be *less involved and more relevant.* Much like being productive and being busy from chapter 4 are not the same thing, neither is being involved and being relevant. Too involved as a leader means getting bogged down in the details of your people's work. Being relevant, on the other hand, means providing high-level direction, allocating resources, shaping the culture of your team, and relentlessly communicating shared purpose. Being involved means working *in* your business. Being relevant means working *on* your business.

Patrick was less involved by not getting into the minutia of his response teams. At the same time, he became more relevant by modeling and shaping a hands-off culture from the top by taking a wide view of the situation and ensuring responsibilities and jurisdictions were understood and respected. He made it clear that the FBI was in charge of the investigation and that the mayor of Boston was "running his streets." Furthermore, the governor knew he could add huge value as a trusted communicator, giving local residents and an international audience hope as the public face of government and serving as a valuable liaison to the White House.

And he continued entering the command center every day asking, "How can I help?"

I certainly hope you will never need to lead through a horrific incident like the Boston Marathon bombing, but there is an important lesson here.

In chaotic environments, leaders often instinctively feel the need to micromanage. Getting involved in details and being asked for approval on lots of decisions confirms our role as leader and makes us feel important, which is something many of us, if we are honest, yearn for.

Yet it is the exact opposite that is required from you as a leader in today's business climate. The world changes rapidly, sometimes by the hour, and your team members often do not have the time it takes to feed a question up the org chart and wait for a response. It may sound counterintuitive, but the faster things move and the more complex your business challenges are, the more authority and control you need to give up and the more you need to delegate and empower.

Strive to become the humble leader who resists the urge to control and approve in order to make you feel important. This is selfish. Empower your people by being *less involved* in the weeds so you have time and energy to be *more relevant* where you are truly needed. When you are, you shift from a content-expert leader to a strategic leader, which is far more powerful because you set, model, and communicate the direction for your team through clarity of shared purpose.

In order to lead this way, you must—as Jim Collins wrote in *Good to Great*[2]—have the right people on the bus and in the right seat and the wrong people off it. Simply giving up control and delegating more can be a dangerous move if your people do not have the necessary skills, knowledge, and sense of perspective to act on it wisely. As a humble leader, you therefore must spend your time and energy on ensuring your staff has the resources they need to get the job done. You must be the humble creator of the right environment for your team.

## "I Get to Decide"

Up to the time of this writing (July 2023), the astonishing success of the Ukraine armed forces in holding back a much larger Russian enemy is a telling example of the power of empowerment by higher-ups giving up control and pushing decision-making down the chain of command. "I get to decide how and when I engage the Russian enemy," said a Ukrainian mechanized infantry company commander. The Ukrainian soldiers and officers are empowered to make frontline decisions and take initiative as they see fit.

Compare this to the Russian army, where, according to interviews with two dozen American, NATO, and Ukrainian officials by the *New York Times*, soldiers are not empowered to make on-the-spot decisions, and the officer corps isn't empowered to take initiative either. The far-too-centralized leadership of the Russian military requires lieutenants to feed decisions all the way up to the generals (and sometimes even the president) and ask permission even on the smallest matters (THEN). It is one of the main reasons why the Russians have struggled in the war against a much more empowered, flexible, and nibble opponent.

The Ukrainians chose highly empowered execution on the front lines and pushed decision-making as low down the chain as possible to give their units lots of room for independent initiatives (NOW), which helped hold off a seemingly overwhelming force.[3]

## NOW Leadership … NOW!
### *Practice Delegating*

Pull up your to-do list. Ask yourself for every item, "Who else can do this?" Then identify one item on your to-do list that you can delegate to someone else this week. Then delegate it to that person.

My one item to delegate this week is _____

to _____.

Make a list of three decisions that you need to make over the course of the next week. Ask yourself for every decision, "Who has the best information to make this call?" Then identify one decision that you can delegate to someone else this week. Then delegate decision-making to that person.

My one decision to delegate this week is _____

to _____.

## Empower with Shared Purpose

To truly empower your people and to delegate to those best suited for the job, your team requires clarity about your shared purpose. When you stop seeking control, you can focus on defining what that shared purpose will be. This gives your whole team valuable direction on what you are all working toward. You shift your team from working for the leader to working for the shared purpose.

For Governor Patrick and the Ukrainian armed forces, the shared purposes were clearly understood: save lives and bring the perpetrators to justice for the former, and defend our home country, no matter the cost in the latter.

Your shared purpose should be simple and tangible with clear marching orders for all your team members. Leading with your hands off through clarity of shared purpose is in this way leading like a compass, showing true north versus providing a detailed map on how to get there.

Here are a few more examples of shared purposes of teams I have been or am a part of:

**Investment advising firm (team size: 60)**
- To empower our clients to invest wisely and live fully.

**Military observer group, Lebanon (team size: 100)**
- To observe, monitor, report, and/or investigate all incidents that are or could lead to a violation of UN Security Council Resolution 1701.

**CEO peer performance group/Vistage model (team size: 12)**
- To support and challenge one another so that we may all reach and exceed our full potential as CEOs.

**Two-man 530-mile Race Across Oregon Team (team size: 8)**
- Safely win the race and beat the course record. Safety=Speed.

**Executive team of the Family Association (or PTA) of my boys'
school (team size: 15)**

- To provide leadership that nurtures a spirit of community between
  the school and its families and among families.

Every team, no matter its size or tenure, needs a shared purpose, and it is
your job as the head to make the shared purpose explicit and then relentlessly
communicate it across your teams.

While the process of arriving at a shared purpose takes some thoughtful-
ness, don't sink too much time into it. Two or three brainstorming sessions
with your team are sufficient. Unlike a vision or a mission, your shared
purpose can change more frequently over time. This is because a shared
purpose gives your team immediate guidance for how to run a specific phase
or project in your business.

---

# NOW Leadership ... NOW!
## *Identifying the "One Thing"*

How do you arrive at a shared purpose? Ask, discuss, and answer this
very simple but powerful question together with your team: What
is the one most important thing we need to do extraordinarily well
around here to win? What is the *one* thing? That one thing becomes
your shared purpose.

I will introduce the concept of shared purpose to my team on
_____ (date)
and then lead a team discussion to arrive at a shared purpose on
_____ (date).

---

## "Stop Doing Anything Stupid, Goofy, or Crazy"

In August 2012, Best Buy was on the brink of bankruptcy. Newly appointed CEO Hubert Joly was under tremendous pressure to prevent disaster and turn the big-box store around. Yet instead of immediately slashing head count and cutting expenses, Joly spent his first week on the job as newly minted CEO working on the floor of a Best Buy store with a name tag that read "CEO in Training."

You might think that's an unconventional if not outright crazy way to spend your first week on the job as the designated turnaround CEO. But Joly knew what he was doing. He knew that this frontline experience would help shape the initial shared purpose for his plan to right the ship. Toward the end of his first week as CEO-in-training—and of course after thorough research and many interviews with people from the front lines up to the C-level—Joly settled on the initial shared purpose: "Let's stop doing anything that's either stupid, goofy, or crazy."

This was it!

Joly realized that before a grand new strategy was called for, the basics needed to get fixed first. As time went on and stupid, goofy, and crazy actions declined, Joly shifted the shared purpose at Best Buy to superior customer service, or as it is still known today, to "service like the Geek Squad." Through a clear shared purpose, he vocally and publicly empowered his knowledgeable Blue Shirts to do the job they were hired to do: delight customers.

In Joly's words, "You empower. If you see something, do something. And it's creating that sense that, yes, I can make a difference. I can create a world around me. Initially you can think that's going to be chaos. No, because if you have this purpose, the values, the principles, clarity about what people are doing, that's how you unleash your magic. It's so beautiful to see. Because there was a point . . . where I said, 'I've actually lost control of this operation. I mean, it's completely out of my hands now.' And that's when the performance started to skyrocket." By empowering his people through a clear shared purpose, Joly helped Best Buy escape bankruptcy and over the course of the next year tripled the value of the stock.[4]

An important lesson from Joly's highly successful turnaround of Best Buy is that when you empower your people, do it publicly. Let your people know loudly, clearly, and often that you trust them. As a result, they will see themselves positively through your eyes and work hard to live up to your expectations.

Another big retailer, Nordstrom, is legendary for empowering its staff through a clear shared purpose of superior customer service. While other retailers have lengthy employee handbooks, Nordstrom's is incredibly simple: It has one page with one rule.[5] You read it when you started this chapter. See table 8.1 for a summary of micromanagement versus lead like a compass.

*Table 8.1: Micromanagement vs. Lead Like a Compass*

| MICROMANAGEMENT | LEAD LIKE A COMPASS |
| --- | --- |
| Tell how to solve problems | Listen, ask good questions |
| Booged down in details | Provide high-level direction, allocate resources |
| Keep information close to the vest | Share with full transparency |
| Need to know it all | Good at not knowing. Curious to learn |
| Control freak | Empowerment freak |
| Create work with unnecessary reports and updates | Informed about what matters |
| "Do this!" | "How can I help?" |
| Be in control and feel needed | Push decision-making as far down as possible |
| Too involved, less relevant | Highly relevant, less involved |
| Working in business | Working on business |
| Lead by approving and controlling | Lead with shared purpose |

## 150 Times, Seven Different Ways

Once you've defined your shared purpose, you must relentlessly communicate and live it by example. It is imperative that everyone on your team have a clear understanding of your shared purpose.

Don't underestimate how hard this is. Study after study reveals how little of what we as leaders communicate actually sticks with our people. For example, in one study, only 25 percent of the people responsible for *executing strategy* could list three of their company's strategic priorities.[6]

Experience has taught me that nothing gets heard unless it's communicated 150 times and seven different ways. OK, I am not claiming that 150 times, seven different ways is based on scientific data, but I don't think I'm far off. I pulled the expression out of you-know-where during my days as a CEO peer group facilitator to make the point that it is impossible to overcommunicate as a leader.

An excellent rule of thumb is this: when you feel like a broken record, when you feel like you cannot bring yourself to communicate the same shared purpose one more time, *and* when you hear your people paraphrase back to you what you are saying, then and only then is your message starting to get heard.

You can help encourage that when you lead by example. When faced with a decision, get into the habit of constantly coming back to the shared purpose. Talk explicitly about how a shared purpose serves as a compass: Does option A or option B serve our shared purpose better? Model this for your people, and make it clear that you expect everyone to use the shared purpose as a guidepost when they are faced with decisions. Make sure to share stories of team members who successfully made independent, smart decisions with the guidepost of the shared purpose. Shine a light on your people who made empowered decisions with the shared purpose as a true North Star.

## How Empowerment Leads to Magic

When your team members have a clear shared purpose and feel trusted to make frontline decisions, magic happens.

Former Ritz-Carlton president Herve Humler shared the story of a fourteen-year-old wheelchair-bound guest who checked in with his family at the Ritz-Carlton in Dubai. Upon looking through the lobby's massive windows, the teenager took one look at the gorgeous beach, turned to his parents, and said, "I sure wish I could swim in that beautiful ocean."

The problem was that between the hotel and the beach stood a two-hundred-meter stretch of sand over which a wheelchair could most certainly not travel.

Within earshot of the family was a hotel maintenance worker who overheard the conversation. The worker paused and thought, *I'm going to do something about this*. She quickly rounded up a few of her maintenance department coworkers, and a mere five hours later, they had completed their masterpiece: a brand-new wooden walkway over the beach that the wheelchair could easily roll over to get down to the water.

For the staff at the Ritz-Carlton Dubai, it was simply another day as part of a team that was empowered to take fast action and make independent decisions. For the teenager, it was the first time he had ever been swimming in the ocean.

Nobody instructed the maintenance worker that she must construct a walkway to the ocean. She did not need the approval from her supervisor either. Instead, Ritz-Carlton has built an empowered culture that challenges each employee to reach for the next level through a shared purpose that the hotel is world-renowned for: top service.[7]

Whether at the Ritz, in a crisis, in the C-suite, in a war zone, or in your own team, you improve internal performance and engage external clients and partners when you become *less involved* and *more relevant*. As you now know from the first Shift (Dig Deep), this requires you as a humble leader to feel secure enough in yourself and your leadership so that you don't feel the need to hold on to control and decisions but can get out of the way and let your teams do the job they were hired to do.

True magic as a humble leader happens when you empower your team by providing them with a clear shared purpose that serves as a compass showing true north.

# CHAPTER 9
# BUILD A LEADERSHIP FACTORY

*Train people well enough so they can leave.*
*Treat them well enough so they don't want to.*
—**Richard Branson**

## How Do You Become a Talent Magnet?

Staring at my computer screen, unable to focus on the scholarly article I was trying to write, I felt the imminent meeting with my professor weighing heavily on me. I had hardly slept the night before. The last thing I wanted to do was disappoint my mentor, but I had difficult news to share with him.

I was twenty-seven years old and had been in my job as a research assistant at the Department of Geography at the University of Zürich in Switzerland for only a few months. I was a PhD student researching snow-related tourism. But I had made a big decision. Having just spent time cross-country ski racing in Australia and traveling that amazing continent (and yes, falling in love with an Aussie girl), I had chosen to pursue an opportunity to conduct fieldwork for my dissertation Down Under (I can confirm there is snow in Australia).

My professor did not yet know it, but I had an invitation to spend up to eighteen months as a visiting scholar at one of the leading environmental research centers at the Australian National University in Canberra. Despite living out of a duffel bag all over the globe for most of the year due to my frequent racing and training as a cross-country skier, I'd never worked and lived outside my home country, Switzerland, aside from a two-year stint in New Zealand as a child. Being able to conduct my fieldwork Down Under would be a dream come true both personally and professionally.

But it meant that I had to quit my job as research assistant only a few months into the job, and I was sure I would disappoint my boss, who had unconditionally supported me through my master's thesis and placed a great deal of confidence in me by hiring me in the first place. I knew loyalty was a big virtue to him. He was committed to his team and expected the same in return. And here I was about to quit on him. I was a notorious people-pleaser back then (something that I have worked hard to get better at over the years), and I was dreading this meeting.

When we finally sat down for lunch and had taken our first sips from our large beer steins (this was Europe in 1993, remember!), I proceeded to share my plans. "I have some good and some bad news."

My professor looked at me expectantly.

"I have an invitation to conduct my fieldwork for my PhD in Australia," I continued. "I am very excited about it, but it would mean I have to quit my job with you here."

"Go on," he said.

"Well, I feel terrible about it and am really torn, but I have decided I would like to go. It would give me a unique opportunity to work overseas."

All my professor said was "I see."

This did not exactly calm my nerves. I kept on sharing my rationale and excitement while continuing to stress how bad I felt about having to quit. I was prepared to have to respond to a massive guilt trip. But to my big surprise, that didn't happen. As the conversation progressed, my professor took a keen interest. He asked a lot of questions about what I would be doing in Australia, the challenges around the fieldwork, the university I would be affiliated with, and, interestingly, my intended return date. To my huge surprise, he not only accepted my decision but supported it wholeheartedly by offering to rehire me when I came back.

I had already perceived my professor as someone who never put himself first. He was a master at elevating all of us on his team, and he took great pride in our successes. Many ambitious academics work their PhD students to death, all in service of their own research, while leaving students with little time to pursue their own interests and studies. I knew he was different because he gave us research assistants a lot of flexibility. It was one of the main reasons I had been so excited to join his team. I knew all this, but I still never expected him to support my leaving so soon to go halfway around the globe.

My research experience in Australia ended up being a big win all around. I was able to produce high-quality original research for my PhD degree, which got a lot of coverage in the Australian national press. That helped the profile of my host, the Australian National University. The benefits extended to my professor's team in Zürich, as my fieldwork enabled us to publish numerous academic papers under the banner of the University of Zürich together.

By supporting me in my crazy idea, my professor was embracing a concept I call a leadership factory. He was keenly aware that very few of his PhD students and research assistants would end up staying in academia, let alone at his university. He therefore made it his goal to challenge and shape us into the next generation of leaders outside the academic world. Or as it was with me: to fully support me in conducting my research on the other side of the world, thereby gaining valuable new academic, cultural, and personal experiences.

## What a Leadership Factory Looks Like

You might feel a bit reluctant to embrace the notion of a leadership factory, as you might be afraid of losing talented people prematurely. Won't people leave your team if you make them even more employable?

The ironic truth is that when you stretch your strong performers, you will keep them longer and better prepare them for their next step. Yes, transforming your team into a leadership factory induces loyalty.

Importantly, when you as leader become known for coaching people toward their next career step, word gets around. As a result, you attract more of the brightest and best. Transforming your team into a leadership factory turns you into a talent magnet because people see a future with you.

It's the right thing to do by your people for their growth and development *and* for building valuable professional relationships with your former team members who move into senior positions in your and other organizations.

One important point to make about the leadership factory is that not everybody wants, or is capable of taking on, a management or higher-level position. There are certainly plenty of outstanding individual contributors (IC) who will remain important to your team even if they don't move up the company ladder.

The leadership factory concept still applies to them, although in a slightly different way. Instead of formally promoting them, be sure they get the recognition they deserve. Maybe they can mentor and teach newer team members in one of their areas of expertise. A great way to "promote" outstanding ICs who are not interested in a vertical move is to designate them as go-to experts or gurus. The more of them your team produces, the higher the number of smart, talented people who will line up to work for you.

When you run a leadership factory, you have the humility to recognize your people won't hang on with you forever. Therefore, you should prepare them for the next level of leadership. You're also exhibiting humility in knowing you will eventually be replaced, too, and that part of your responsibility is to answer the crucial question, Who will take my job?

## NOW Leadership ... NOW!
### Initiate Check-In Conversations

Start holding regular career-path meetings with each of our team members. Simply grab a cup of coffee and have a chat. Start with "Karen, it's been a while since we talked about your career goals. Are you still thinking about ..."

During check-in conversations, you may ask the following questions:

- Where do you see yourself in one year? Three years? Five years?
- How can you achieve this here?
- What do you need to learn? Who do you need to know?
- What parts of your job are most interesting and rewarding?
- What areas are you finding most challenging?
- What are you doing to reach short- and long-term career goals?
- What are other projects, task forces, or additional responsibilities you would like to be a part of?
- What are you curious about that you haven't explored yet?
- How can I best support your professional development?

The person I will hold the first career-path meeting with is _____ .
I will get this done by _____ .

Turning your team into a leadership factory enables you to let go and lead like a compass. When you train the next generation of workers who are willing and able to take on more responsibility for the organization, you are setting the stage for what we talked about in the last chapter. You build capacity to free yourself from the day-to-day running of your business and become less involved so you can help define the North Star.

I often take this notion a step further by challenging my executive coaching and speaking clients to make themselves obsolete. That's right—make yourself obsolete. Work yourself out of a job. Build a strong talent pool that enables you to delegate and empower in all key phases of the organization so your presence is not required for the day-to-day running of your business.

In his excellent book *The Culture Code: The Secrets of Highly Successful Groups*,[1] Daniel Coyle shares how leaders of highly successful teams have a habit of leaving their teams alone during certain key situations to foster initiative and engagement. For example, about once per month, Gregg Popovich of the San Antonio Spurs, one of the most successful basketball coaches in NBA history, never walks over to his players during a timeout.

The players sit on the bench waiting for him until they realize he is not coming. Then they take charge and figure out a plan together.

Similarly, the New Zealand All Blacks rugby team runs several practices each week with little or no input from the coaches. And the best Special Operator SEAL teams are those that over time learned to rely very little on their formal instructor and instead have figured out among themselves what they need to learn and train.

As I've already shared from personal experience, the ultimate test of leadership is how the ship sails when you are not there.

Many leaders become so defined by their role, they find it difficult to envisage a future in which they are no longer in charge. That's not my view! If you have the humility to know you are replaceable (and you're fooling yourself if you believe otherwise), you might as well drive the process of succession planning. Turning your team into a leadership factory is the best approach to doing that.

Take Mastercard, for example. In 2009, Mastercard had to hire a new CEO in the midst of the financial crisis. Part of the hiring conversation between then chairman of the board, Rick Haythornthwaite, and the external CEO candidate, Ajay Banga, was—believe it or not—not just the immediate CEO succession but also the next one.

Before Ajay even had the job, they were talking about a rough timeline of ten years for his tenure and imagining his replacement. They both expressed a strong desire not to hire from the outside next time around. This mutual forward-thinking cemented their match. Ajay got the job and over the next decade tripled revenue and grew market cap tenfold. After a thoughtful and deliberate succession planning process, in 2020 Ajay handed the reins to Mastercard veteran executive Michael Miebach. Ajay started his tenure as CEO with the goal of replacing himself. So should you.[2]

Here is one additional but often forgotten (slightly self-serving) benefit of preparing your own successor. If you want to get promoted yourself, you increase your chances at promotion by having a strong candidate in place to backfill your job when you move on to greener pastures. I have been part of many discussions with executive teams who were looking at filling an open role. Everything else being equal, having your own successor lined up will put you at a clear advantage. It saves the executive team the headache of finding *your* replacement.

## NOW Leadership ... NOW!
### *Clarify Your Team's Career Aspirations*

Mentally scan your team and ask yourself:

1.  How clear are you on what each person's career aspirations are?
2.  What potential do you see in them (guru, one-up manager)?
3.  Is there a disconnect between #1 and #2? Why? If there is a disconnect, do they know?
4.  What is their number one area for growth, and how can you challenge and support them?

During your next one-on-one meetings, talk through these questions with each of your team members.

## Don't Fret over the People You Lose

Leadership factories prove to be an advantage even when your A-players leave and seed other organizations. As they transform into leaders in the divisions of large corporations, they can become de facto ambassadors for your cause and also people you can reach out to for help (the ambassador effect).

In small businesses, they move on to lead other businesses—the same businesses you can then lean on when you may need guidance or that will become your customers (the new client effect). In addition, if you stretch and support your people, they are more likely to return (the boomerang effect).

## The Boomerang Effect

Some of your good people might leave only to realize that the new job wasn't exactly what they had hoped for or that the new company culture wasn't the right fit. Others might give the start-up world a go, which of course is notorious for its high failure rate.

Sooner or later, these great employees may be looking for work again, and you want to be at the top of their list. In a volatile work environment, these "boomerang" employees are on the rise. A recent study found that more than a quarter of all "new" hires are in fact boomerang employees who had resigned within the last thirty-six months.[3] Hiring managers view them as an increasingly valuable source of talent, in part due to the tight labor market but also because they are a known entity.

The farewell party for an employee may turn out to have been merely "farewell for now." When you part ways on a high note because you treated them well by challenging and mentoring them as part of your leadership factory team, you help them feel that leaving is something like leaving their work "home." It's not unusual for people to want to return "home" someday.

By helping your team members improve and excel, you are creating a valuable network of alumni who may come full circle in the future. And even if they don't return, they become valuable brand ambassadors for your organization.[4]

## The Ambassador Effect

My client Mary ran the operations of a retail chain in Australia. Mary was a tough but tender boss. She elevated standards while building meaningful, cooperative relationships with her team members. She constantly challenged her team members to strive for the next level. Mary loved her team but was often frustrated with the highly bureaucratic and hierarchical way the business was organized. She found it incredibly difficult to work across departments. Just getting the simplest piece of information from other teams was tedious and difficult.

When Johanna, one of her strongest-performing reports, was considered for a senior role in the finance department, Mary unconditionally supported her application, even though she knew she would have to hire and onboard someone new, and that would cost her time and energy. She took great pride in her people's success, so when Johanna landed the job, Mary was delighted for her—but also for her team.

Why? Now, whenever Mary or her team needed something from finance, they could simply pick up the phone, call their beloved former team member, and get what they needed immediately instead of having to go through notoriously painful and slow regular channels. Further, Johanna took active steps within her new finance department to make life for Mary's team easier. In the process, she became Mary's ambassador.

## NOW Leadership … NOW!
### *Watch Out for That Bus!*

Ask yourself this morbid question: If I get hit by the infamous bus tomorrow, who would take my job? Once you've identified that person, have a conversation with them and immediately start to transfer tasks and responsibilities (small at first, and gradually more important ones) to them.

Who will do my job? _____

My first three tasks to transfer:

1. _____

2. _____

3. _____

Bonus: As part of this conversation, start to document your responsibilities and procedures that help to ensure your team's institutional memory is well in place and broad based enough that your team will thrive if something unexpected were to happen to you tomorrow.

## The New Client Effect

Meredith, another client, owns a small business in the fashion design industry. Over the last few years, she steadily grew the business until she was finally able to build a strong management team.

Judy, who had been with Meredith since the founding of the business, was her lead designer and a key person on the management team. Over the years Meredith had worked hard on preparing Judy for that lead design role on the management team. Judy was a star performer, and Meredith relied on her a great deal. When Judy decided to go out on her own and start her own gig, Meredith was understandably disappointed. She also fretted somewhat about the hiring and training of Judy's successor. Nevertheless, Meredith and Judy remained close, and Meredith was more than happy to help Judy out with entrepreneurial advice whenever she needed it.

Was Judy's leaving just a one-sided net loss for Meredith? Not at all. When it came time for Judy's business to purchase crucial fabrics, she called Meredith. Meredith's business was one of the first suppliers for Judy's newly opened business, and as Judy's business grew, so did the orders for Meredith's product. Today, Judy is one of Meredith's largest clients. Meredith's leadership factory approach was the right thing to do by Judy, and it paid off on her own bottom line as well.

Some entrepreneurs and business owners let their ego lead the way by getting upset when strong employees leave their "work family." These leaders fall to the temptation to punish the departing person by cutting ties, which inevitably only hurts themselves. Not only do they miss out on the potential long-term benefits of a boomerang, ambassador, or new client, but they also set an example that paints them in a negative light to those who stay on. You can bet that behavior affects how those who stay on view their relationship with the boss going forward.

As much as it may hurt, put ego aside and stay connected. See figure 9.1 for a summary of the benefits of building a leadership factory.

*Figure 9.1: The Benefits of a Leadership Factory Checklist*

- ✅ Free yourself up from the day-to-day grind
- ✅ Build capacity to delegate more
- ✅ Increase chances for your own promotion
- ✅ Boomerang Effect
- ✅ Ambassador Effect
- ✅ New Client Effect
- ✅ Create a portfolio of strong leaders as your legacy

## My Professor: A Postscript

When you build your team into a leadership factory, you will attract and grow the best and brightest. This builds capacity for you as a humble leader to empower and delegate comprehensibly, allowing you to step away from the day-to-day and lead like a compass.

Almost all the senior leaders in the later stages of their careers whom I know and have worked with take great pride and satisfaction in the successes of their former leadership factory employees. As one dear friend and former client put it to me, "Their success and track record become part of my legacy, and I am immensely proud of that legacy."

This is true also for my professor whom you met at the opening of this chapter. After my return from the research stay in Australia back to my home university in Zürich and for many more years, I observed numerous fellow PhDs experience the same benefits of my professor's leadership factory approach.

All of them were elevated to the next level. Many of his former PhD students now hold senior positions in government, business, politics, and academia. Our professor is immensely proud of all of us. And despite his advanced age of eighty, once per year, humble leader Professor Elsasser—or as we know him, Hans—gets his former PhD students together for a reunion.

# RADICAL HUMILITY

## (THEN) to (NOW)

| What Radical Humility Is Not (THEN) | What Radical Humility Is (NOW) |
| --- | --- |
| Insecure | Confident |
| Indifferent | Ambitious |
| Wavering | Decisive |
| Hero leader: I know | Learning leader: good at not knowing |
| Individual wins | Team wins |
| I tell | I ask |
| Inflated ego | Accurate view of myself |
| Self-promote | Self-reflect |
| Leadership development is touchy-feely | Leadership is a contact sport |
| I listen to tell | I listen to learn |
| Try to do it all | Focus |
| It's all important | Only a few things really matter |
| Rushed ignorance | Thoughtful deliberation |
| Avoid taking risks | Embrace failure as learning |
| Dwell on failures | Look ahead |
| Fixed mindset | Growth mindset |
| Transactional relationships | Giving a damn about your people |

| What Radical Humility Is Not (THEN) | What Radical Humility Is (NOW) |
| --- | --- |
| Human resources | See each team member as a whole person |
| Build relationships to be "nice" | Build relationships with a business purpose |
| Tear others down | Build others up |
| Deliver tough feedback in a tough way | Deliver tough feedback in a humane way |
| Low standards | High standards |
| Need control | Provide clarity |
| Micromanage | Empower |
| I need to be more involved | I am more relevant |
| Bogged down in details | Provide high-level direction, allocate resources |
| I want the credit | I share the spotlight |
| Tightly hang on to your best people | Embrace losing your best people |
| It's all about me | It's all about the team |
| I am irreplaceable | I make myself obsolete |

Scan the QR code below for materials that will help you integrate Shift III: Lead Like a Compass into your daily life:

- reprintable figures
- reprintable tables
- all NOW Leadership . . . NOW prompts from Shift III consolidated in one place
- bonus content—research, quotes, tool kits, and exercises that will help you lead like a compass

## DIMENSIONS

**Self-Knowledge/
Growth Mindset**

# SHIFT I
# DIG DEEP

# SHIFT II
# TOUGH ON RESULTS,
# TENDER ON PEOPLE

# SHIFT III
# LEAD LIKE A COMPASS

**Leading
Relationally (Team)/
Growth Mindset**

# SHIFT IV
# FULL TRANSPARENCY

**Leading
Relationally (Org.)/
Growth Mindset**

# SHIFT V
# CHAMPION A
# FEARLESS CULTURE

|  | THEN | | NOW |
|---|---|---|---|
| | Blind spot | | Self-awareness |
| | Trying to do it all |  | Laser-sharp focus |
| | Personal failure as a loss | | Failing successfully |
| | Transactional relationships at work |  | Strong personal relationships at work |
| | Feedback that tears down | | Feedback that builds up |
| | Micromanagement | → | Front-line empowerment |
| | Talent shortage | | Talent magnet |
| | False hero, knows-it-all façade | → | Trust through vulnerability |
| | Avoidance, secrecy | | Openness, honesty |
| | Afraid to speak up; hide, cover up mistakes |  | Psychological safety |
| | Fear-driven culture | | Fearless culture |

**HUMBLE LEADERSHIP = NOW LEADERSHIP**

# SHIFT IV
# FULL TRANS-PARENCY

## Humbly Asking the Big Questions:

1. How do you build trust with vulnerability?
2. How do you model and insist on more honesty and openness?

We live in a world where vast amounts of data—whether expert insights, in-depth research, or idle gossip—are available to anyone at the click of a button. A single smartphone video can bring down or elevate a brand within seconds. There is no hiding. And it's not just social media. There are more information and opinions about everything under the sun than ever before.

We've already discussed that your employees need to make smart, fast decisions independently instead of waiting for top-down direction. And for them to make thoughtful and fast decisions on the front lines, they need to know more about management's strategy, business goals, and intentions.

The only way they'll know more is if you as a leader share more—and that requires full transparency.

Leaders must be open not just about their goals and rationales but also their imperfections. Say goodbye to creating an illusion of the infallible perfect hero who single-handedly rises to the top. Instead, embrace your shortcomings. In Shift I (Dig Deep), you learned about the importance of knowing thyself by becoming more self-aware as a leader, being willing to accept your imperfections, and embracing your personal failures as an opportunity for growth.

This Shift is taking it a step further by inviting you to share your intentions, goals, and imperfections with full transparency with others—for the greater benefit of your team and organization. Share honestly where you suck.

In this Shift, you will learn (1) how to build trust with your people by sharing your shortcomings with vulnerability and (2) how to lead with full transparency by sharing more or everything.

# CHAPTER 10
# HERE IS WHERE I SUCK

*I now wish to make the personal acknowledgment*
*that you were right, and I was wrong.*
—**Abraham Lincoln, sixteenth US president**
**(in a letter to General Ulysses S. Grant)**

## How Do You Build Trust with Vulnerability?

"Hello, everybody. Thank you all for participating in my 360 survey. I was glad to read that you appreciate my strengths as a highly driven leader with strong analytical skills. I also received the feedback that you see me as outstanding at project execution and as having a deep passion for the business."

My executive coaching client Michelle took a deep breath before continuing to address the small group of attendees that included her boss, her whole team, and some of her peers. It was her executive coaching kickoff meeting, and Michelle was just getting started.

"I also learned that I have numerous things I need to work on and improve. You see me at times as overly competitive and too aggressive and controlling. You also told me that I can come across as arrogant and emotionally volatile with not a lot of appreciation for personal relationships."

The bored, passive expressions on many faces changed to disbelief. Dead silence. Some glanced at one another with "can you believe she just said that?" looks on their faces, but Michelle continued, undaunted.

"I must be honest with you. Receiving this feedback has not been easy, and since receiving the written report a week ago, I have gone through a range of emotions, mostly negative ones. But after talking it over with my coach and my husband and some close friends, I can now accept it. I want to get better. So the first thing I want to do is offer an apology to all those I have hurt with my behavior. It is very obvious to me now that I can get carried away at times and that I leave collateral damage along the way. I am sorry."

Michelle took a sip of water before finishing.

"And the second thing I want to tell you is that I intend to turn over a new leaf today. I am committed to getting better. To show you how serious I am about this, I will share the results of my 360 and my coaching goals with all of you via email. Thank you again for your willingness to participate and help me to get better. I will now hand it over to my coach, Urs, who will talk a bit more about the process."

We wrapped up the meeting, and as people got ready to leave, I observed numerous folks making a point of shaking Michelle's hand and thanking her for her honesty and transparency. The same afternoon, Michelle received an email from her boss that read, "Dear Michelle, well done today in the coaching kickoff meeting. You displayed a lot of humility. That requires guts. I believe this will go a long way with the team. Keep up the great work. Looking forward to participating in your coaching process. Best, Dan."

Fast-forward nine months to the end of our coaching engagement. When I conducted my routine anonymous survey at the end of the engagement with Michelle's team, her boss, and peers, they clearly assessed her as having improved on her coaching goals. They now saw her as less controlling and delegating more. She was seen as someone who invested more time and energy into building personal relationships, and while she was by no means perfect, her emotional outbursts were few and far between.

What all team members without exception appreciated most (and my guess is to this day have not forgotten) was Michelle's display of vulnerability during the initial coaching kickoff meeting.

## The Perfect Façade Crumbles

Many leaders still view vulnerability as a weakness. They believe they need to have all the answers. Because they want to know it all, they require all information flow through them and feel the need to sign off on even the smallest decisions. As a result, they slow progress at every turn.

Even if leaders understand the futility of controlling everything, and even if they believe that displaying vulnerability can be valuable, they are often afraid to share out of fear of losing respect.

But times are changing. Brené Brown, bestselling author and in-demand speaker, has brought vulnerability into the mainstream and popularized it in the business world. Brown defines vulnerability as showing up as your true self while constantly looking at getting better. She defines chasing perfection as focused on, "What will others think?" while an appropriate self-focus is asking, "How can I get better?"[1]

Chasing perfection is often coupled with a fixed mindset, which we discussed in chapter 5. It can lead to sweeping your faults under the rug so you can avoid embarrassment in the short run, but it often results in huge failure over the long haul. Further, if you pretend to have all the answers and are reluctant to admit mistakes or ask for help, your team members will adopt the same approach.

Our actions always speak louder than words, and because leaders cast a long shadow, your behavior will be mirrored. An organization rife with people who don't own up to their mistakes or shortcomings is not meeting its potential.

Thankfully, high-profile leaders are avoiding the trap of chasing perfection and are starting to embrace vulnerability. Microsoft CEO Satya Nadella resurrected the tech giant by transforming its culture from the aggressive command-and-control Steve Ballmer era to a culture based on his own core values: humility, curiosity, and constant learning.[2] Oprah Winfrey, whom we met earlier, became the first Black female billionaire thanks to a highly successful entrepreneurial career that put vulnerability and self-awareness at the center.[3]

Jacinda Ardern, former prime minister of New Zealand, took an empathetic yet firm approach to handling the Christchurch terrorist attack and the early stages of the COVID-19 pandemic to propel her party to historic successes and elevate her to rock-star status. On many occasions, Ardern has opened up with vulnerability to the public about her family (she gave birth while she was in office) and her life outside of governing the country.

Her statement to reporters on her decision to step down in February 2023 after five and a half years in office perfectly encapsulates Radical Humility: "I am leaving because with such a privileged role comes responsibility. The responsibility to know when you are the right person to lead, and also, when you are not . . . I know what this job takes, and I know that I no longer have enough in the tank to do it justice. It is that simple."[4]

## Why Vulnerability?

Business—and life—today demands constant learning and mental agility. No one person can know it all the time—or ever. If you ignore this reality, your blind spots will be exposed. The most respected, successful leaders are those who are aware of their own limitations and share them with vulnerability. In the process, they create sincere, trusting connections with their team members (table 10.1).

As a humble leader, you must

- be more interested in getting it right versus being right,
- not be afraid to admit you are wrong,
- welcome feedback, input, and even criticism—not because you like it any more than the rest of us but because you know it's necessary to make progress individually and lead more effectively—and
- create a culture in which blind spots are identified and constant development is encouraged and rewarded.

Brad Smith exemplified this perfectly when he was the CEO of the financial technology company Intuit. "I actually told the board I wanted to do a 360 assessment and share the results with them, my executive team, and then with the entire company," he said. Smith even taped his 360 results on the door of his office so everyone could see it.

"Each year I created clear development goals that I shared with other rising stars in the leadership pipeline. This created a safe space for them to become more reflective and self-aware. People started checking their egos at the door and asking for help."[5]

You might not tape your 360 to your door yet, but here is one small step you can take. Get in the habit of asking your team members at the end of each one-on-one about your performance as a leader: "What feedback do you have for me? What do you wish I would start doing or stop doing?" By doing this regularly, you normalize asking for and providing feedback.

Employing this strategy, I have received lots of valuable feedback over the course of my career. Some of it helped me grow my leadership skills, but probably 90 percent of what I heard were seemingly small things bugging my team members that I could easily fix before they became bigger issues. For example, early in my first peacekeeping deployment, when returning from the field, if I was in a rush, I would just drop my belt with my sidearm onto my desk and start to work at my computer. But times had changed, and the strict rule now was that the weapon must be worn on your body or locked up.

Old habits die hard, and I continued to simply drop my weapon on my desk as I had done years ago. One of my young officers shared my negligence with me when I invited feedback. I am thankful he did, and it was an easy thing for me to change.

*Table 10.1: Hero Leader vs. Vulnerable Leader*

| Hero Leader | Vulnerable Leader |
| --- | --- |
| Sign off on every decision | Empower and delegate to the right level |
| Bottleneck | Force multiplier |
| Protect perfect façade | Show up as true self, invite feedback |
| Fixed mindset | Growth mindset |
| "What will others think?" | "How can I get better?" |

| Hero Leader | Vulnerable Leader |
|---|---|
| Difficult to admit mistakes | Models how to take responsibility |
| Wants to be right | Wants to get it right |
| Creates a culture of protecting egos | Creates a culture of learning and growing |
| Shuts out feedback | Invites feedback |

# NOW Leadership ... NOW!

## *Prompts to Get Honest Feedback*

Ask these questions during your next one-on-one to invite meaningful feedback you can put to use:

- Where do you want me more involved in your work? Where do you want me less involved?
- What can I do to make your job easier?
- How can I best support you?
- What are we currently doing as a team that you believe we should not be doing?
- What should we be doing instead?
- What is most difficult about this project for you and how can I/ the team help?

The one question I will ask during the next one-on-one is: _____

_____

## Vulnerability First, Trust Second

When I kick off the facilitation of a team retreat or start a team coaching engagement, I often use the "penny exercise" to help people share something personal with vulnerability.

Every person receives a penny. Then I ask them to share a significant event or experience that shaped them into who they are today during the year that is imprinted on the penny, either personally or professionally.

I am always amazed how a group of people who have worked together, many for a long time, discovers something new and personal about one another and how people become closer after impactful things are shared. When participants share an important event from their childhood (such as losing a sibling or getting kicked out of school) or from their adult life (such as a painful divorce or feeling lost professionally), they display vulnerability.

In the spirit of leading by example, I always ask the most senior person in the room to kick it off for the team. The vulnerability displayed by the leader is then almost always mirrored by the rest of the team, which starts a *vulnerability loop*[6]:

1. The leader sends a signal of vulnerability.
2. Team members detect the signal and respond by signaling their own vulnerability.
3. The leader detects the signals.
4. A norm of higher vulnerability is established; closeness and trust increase.

Establishing the vulnerability loop at the kickoff builds the base for deeper trust and closer connection within the team and makes for a more productive session.

This is very important but often misunderstood: we don't need to have trust to show up with vulnerability, but showing up with vulnerability is one of the quickest ways to develop trust with your team. Put another way, trust does not come before vulnerability; vulnerability comes before trust.

Admitting your shortcomings and mistakes, while scary, is refreshing to your team and plants the seed for trust to grow.

## The Fastest Route to Trust

How quickly do you think vulnerability can build deep trust? How about forty-five minutes? In his book *Humbitious: The Power of Low-Ego, High-Drive Leadership*,[7] Amer Kaissi cites a remarkable study in which complete strangers were brought into a lab and divided into pairs. Each pair was assigned to a separate room and then needed to ask and answer specific questions for forty-five minutes.

The first group of pairs was tasked with asking each other small-talk questions such as "Where are you from?" and "What was your favorite subject in school?" The second group had to ask and respond to more meaningful questions that were intended for participants to display vulnerability such as "If you knew that in one year you would die suddenly, would you change anything about the way you are now living? Why?" or "What do love and friendship mean to you?"

Participants in the second group were also asked to alternate sharing something they consider a positive characteristic of their assigned partner.

The study found that participants in the second group formed significantly deeper bonds with one another than the first group. Some formed long-lasting friendships, and one pair even got married! When asked to rate the closeness of the relationships they formed, participants in the second group rated their bond with their partner of forty-five minutes about as close as the average relationship with other people in their lives. Amazingly, some even rated their bond at the level they have with the closest person in their lives.

The takeaway for you is this: Sharing with vulnerability even for *brief periods* of time is one of the most powerful ways to form trusting relationships with your team members fast.

## Vulnerability Is No Replacement for Competence

Denise's business just lost a major account that made up about a third of her business's revenue. How should Denise, the owner-operator, address her team with appropriate vulnerability?

> **Option 1:** "This is terrible news. I am scared and have no idea what to do about it. I really can't believe it. The account team really should have done a better job."

> **Option 2:** "This is terrible news. It scares all of us, including me. I want to discuss with you how we can quickly pivot. I will need all your best thinking and hard work, and I am here to support each and every one of you."

In option 1, Denise is attempting to be vulnerable, but not appropriately so. Team members hear that Denise is lost, overwhelmed, and doesn't know what to do. They hear that it was the account team's fault. They probably feel that she is not fit to lead the team.

In option 2, Denise acknowledges with appropriate vulnerability the strong emotions she and the team are feeling. She makes it clear that she and the team will need to rely on one another to recover and achieve their goals. And she clearly signals that she is strong and capable enough to lead the team out of the conundrum.

The research-backed evidence for more vulnerability in leadership is verified time after time. Let me be clear, though, that showing up with vulnerability is no replacement for competence. If you cost your company millions by ignoring the trends of your industry, for example, no amount of sharing is going to make the team want to follow you. And vulnerability might not always be called for immediately.

When starting out in a new position, sometimes it might not be a great idea to share your insecurities and weaknesses right off the bat. You might first need to "earn your right" to display vulnerability with strong deliverables. This is especially true if

- the organizational culture is autocratic, top-down, and hierarchical;
- your boss and your team members have been used to leaders who need to have all the answers and are reluctant to show weakness; or
- there are open questions about your qualifications for the position.

Use these considerations as a guidepost for how quickly you display vulnerability when starting a new position.

## But Don't Overshare

Humble leadership means a willingness to be transparent, but it also means knowing how not to overshare.

You have to be aware of what is relevant. I don't necessarily need to tell you all about the fight I had with my teenage son last night, but I do need to tell you what I am learning about our new customer and what I am hearing about our competition. You must be thoughtful about determining what is appropriate and helpful and what isn't.

As a humble leader, you are a competent, strong, *and* vulnerable leader. You know how to bring appropriate moods and energy to different situations and people. You understand that you can display varying degrees of vulnerability with different people without being fake. It's not black and white. It never is. It's a balancing act. That is why leadership is a thinking person's sport (table 10.2).

## NOW Leadership ... NOW!
### *Prompts to Start a Vulnerable Conversation*

Use these openers to start a conversation with vulnerability:

- "One of the things I am working on getting better at is ..."
- "I am very curious and have a lot to learn about ..."

- "I feel I did not do very well in that meeting/interaction/discussion/presentation. What do you think?"
- "I think I am off base here. Can you tell me why?"
- "We all have blind spots. Can you please tell me mine?"
- "Let me tell you what I am struggling with professionally ... What are you struggling with professionally?"
- "Tell me what's wrong with this idea." Or "Who can poke some holes into this idea?"
- "This is just my two cents ..."
- "What am I missing here?"

The vulnerable conversation opener that I will use this week is: _____

*Table 10.2: Dos and Don'ts of Vulnerable Leadership*

| DO | DON'T |
|---|---|
| Share what's relevant | Overshare |
| Become comfortable not knowing and learning | Feel the need to have all the answers |
| Relentlessly learn and grow | Believe vulnerability is a replacement for competence |
| Set the tone by going first | Let your team members go first |
| Display varying degrees of vulnerability with different people and in different situations | Display same level of vulnerability with all people and in every situation |

## "Rank Switched Off, Humility Switched On"

"I screwed up pretty badly. I know it, and I am sorry. Here is what I am taking away as lessons so I will do much better next time . . ."

These were the words of one of my commanding officers (CO) at an after-action review (AAR) during my UN peacekeeping mission to the Middle East.

The most constructive AARs in the military are the ones where the highest-ranking officer starts out and humbly shares what they did poorly, much like my CO did. I found it is often the most competent officers who have the courage and confidence to go first, acknowledge their mistakes, and, in the process, model the sort of vulnerability they expect from their team.

My CO's matter-of-fact way of: (1) owning her mistake, (2) apologizing for it while not dwelling on it, and (3) vowing to do better based on her learnings made all team members feel safe to do the same. This particular AAR led to better operations going forward—and isn't that the goal of all this anyway? We can't change the past, but we absolutely can improve what we do and how we are in the future. All that happened because the CO displayed vulnerability by owning her mistake first.

When you lead with Radical Humility, you take responsibility for everything that happens in your team and organization. Even if it is not directly your own fault, you as a leader need to own it. Don't fall into the trap of making excuses or rationalizing poor performance. Don't blame the market, the lack of resources, or your poorly trained people. At the end of the day, full responsibility rests with you and only you.

Dave Cooper, commander of the Navy SEAL team that killed Osama bin Laden, puts it this way in Daniel Coyle's previously mentioned book *The Culture Code: The Secrets of Highly Successful Groups*: "It's got to be safe to talk. Rank switched off and humility switched on. You're looking for that moment where people can say, 'I screwed that up.' In fact, I'd say those might be the most important four words any leader can say: *I screwed that up*."[8]

He goes on to say, "When we talk about courage, we think it's going against the enemy with a machine gun. The real courage is seeing the truth and speaking the truth to one another. People never want to be the person who says, 'Wait a second, what's really going on here?' But inside the squadron, that *is* the culture, and that's why we're successful . . . The squadron succeed because they understand that being vulnerable together is the only way that the team can become invulnerable."[9]

## Start Small

Despite overwhelming evidence for the benefits of vulnerability, it can be scary to actually live it as a leader. That's perfectly normal. But research shows how practicing small acts of vulnerability will reduce that anxiety.[10]

My advice to you, then, is to start small.

## NOW Leadership . . . NOW
### *Little Things Make a Big Difference*

- At the next team meeting, apologize to your team for one mistake you made last week. It doesn't have to be something big; maybe it was just a small error or misunderstanding. Own it, apologize for it (don't rationalize or justify!), and move on.

  Mistake I will apologize for at the next team meeting: _____

  _____

- Next time in a discussion or debate when you don't know the answer or have a solution, say so. Then make it clear how you and your team plan to come up with an answer.

- During your next one-on-one with one of your team members, share one thing that you are working on improving, personal or professional. It does not have to be something huge or foundational. Maybe simply that you work on being more present with your family on the weekends or that you are revamping your time management system at work.

- I will share with _____

  that I am working on improving _____


Train your vulnerability muscle by starting with these small but significant steps and then build from there. While the start can be hard, the upside is huge: when you show up with appropriate vulnerability, you create better relationships with your team members and build and deepen trust quickly. And bettering relationships with your people is, as you by now know, one of the core elements of humble leadership. When you deepen relationships with your people, they will be more motivated to go the extra mile for you and the organization.

All this leads to better business results and stronger outcomes for you and your team.

# CHAPTER 11
## SHARE THE TRUTH

*The miracle is this—the more we share, the more we have.*
—**Leonard Nimoy, as Spock in *Star Trek***

### How Do You Model Honesty and Insist on Openness?

I banged my fist on the table and got up from my chair.

"Goddammit!"

I interrupted one of my best team members, looked at him sternly, and said with a raised voice, "Now it's your time to shut up and listen!"

I got the attention of my whole team. It was 2017, and we had been working together for nine long months during our peacekeeping tour in Kosovo. In that whole time, I had never raised my voice. Now, four days before the end of the mission, I appeared to be losing it. But I had a plan—to raise my voice in a deliberate way, like how I introduced in chapter 7.

I had summoned my team on a Sunday off for an unannounced meeting at 1400 hours because what had been going down over the past few weeks was unacceptable.

A strong team spirit had been established and maintained for most of the tour, but a few weeks earlier, with mission fatigue setting in, I started to observe petty, hurtful behavior. People were saying negative things behind their team members' backs rather than seeking open dialogue. They were avoiding one another rather than collaborating. It wasn't as though they were actively sabotaging, but the passive-aggressive behavior was counter-productive and keeping the unit from being at its best.

Astonishingly, it came from almost all my team members, including my very best ones. I understood why. We were nearing the end of our tour. Everybody was exhausted from living and working on top of one another 24-7. It seemed everybody just wanted to wrap it up and go home. While I understood the urge (I had it too), as their commander I could not accept it.

Reflecting on what to do about it, I remembered one of the important principles I had been taught early in my mountaineering, endurance athlete, and military careers: accidents happen when the main push is over and people let down their guards. They relax and lose focus.

It's true in mountaineering when people often forget that coming down is much more dangerous than going up. It happens in ultraraces when driving home after an exhausting and sleep-deprived race. And it's true in the military when shooting accidents often happen after the main exercise is over. As leaders, it is our responsibility to model, demand, and—if necessary—force focus until the very last minute.

Shifting to an earnest but direct tone, I outlined to my team some of the destructive behaviors I'd observed. I normalized *the feeling* of mission fatigue but stressed the importance of following through and focusing to the very end.

"We don't want to jeopardize our strong performance and track record with a dumb or potentially dangerous error over the last few days," I said. "As I have said all along, you don't have to be best friends, but you must be able to work together . . . and work together well."

I continued.

"Here is what you will do now: you will speak with everyone on our team one-on-one for fifteen minutes. During that time, you will tell each other honestly what's bothering you about the other person. And that includes me. All the stuff I overheard over the past few weeks, I want you to share it with each other and me. We will now take three hours to get this done. After that, you will have the evening off. My expectation is this: tomorrow morning, from the minute we get up, we will be focused on finishing our mission strong as ONE TEAM. Oh, and one more thing: These fifteen-minute conversations are not a request; they are a direct order. Dismissed."

My team followed through and did what I asked them to do. I could tell the majority did not like it one bit, but behavior over the last few days improved significantly, and we regrouped to finish our tour strongly.

As you can tell, I showed up purposefully with a little tantrum to send a signal. I really forced open communication. I am not advocating for demanding unwanted, uncomfortable sharing in most situations. But with time running out, the finish line in sight, and safety concerns on my mind, I felt it an appropriate approach to take. There is no doubt in my mind that the main reason why my aggressive approach worked and why my team members took it seriously was because we had built meaningful, trusting relationships over the previous nine months.

I was not just some green officer yelling at them. I had been their boss for nine intense months—a boss whom they had worked well with, whom they had laughed (and sometimes cried) with, and whom they trusted. They had not had to grow accustomed to me barking in their faces every day like a drill sergeant at boot camp. If they had, they would have tuned me out.

My shift in tone was sincere and surprising; it got their attention. The strong relationship we had built gave me the license to force honesty.

## Inspiring Openness

Forcing openness must be the exception. Instead, you want to inspire it by taking proactive steps to share more with people and have them share more with you and with one another. Here's why:

> **Healthier team dynamic and culture:** When hard things remain unsaid and are allowed to fester, passive-aggressive behavior and drama rise. Full transparency allows for difficult, even fierce, conversations so people can air their grievances. Ideally, the issues can be resolved, but even if that is not possible, at least your team members will know they've been heard. Open communication will kill the elephant in the room for the benefit of everybody.

**Meet business imperatives:** For your team to stay competitive, people need to understand how their work as an individual is part of the team's overall goal and organizational purpose. To get there, you need to share more with your people, and all teams in your organization need to share more with each other.

When you read these examples that follow, consider how full transparency provides proactive steps to ensure the truth is shared. Whether to improve your team culture or enhance business performance (or often, both), your job as leader is to model and insist on (and in rare cases, force) openness and honesty.

## Share Uncomfortable Truths

Paul entered Laura's office and slowly and deliberately closed the door.

"Have you heard about the payroll spreadsheet?" he said.

Laura looked at him puzzled, completely unaware.

"HR accidentally sent the employee payroll to everyone in the company!"

Laura's eyes widened. "No," she gasped.

"Yes."

Laura immediately turned to her monitor and opened her email. Sure enough, there it was, an all-company email with the attachment "Employee Salary Spreadsheet." Laura double-clicked to open it. Paul got up to see.

"Brian is making fifteen thousand dollars more than me even though he has less experience?" Laura exclaimed.

Paul chimed in: "And look, Briana is making twenty thousand dollars more than me even though she does not have P&L responsibility. I cannot believe this."

The same scene was playing out all over the company. Needless to say, the next few weeks were not pleasant as the whole staff stewed over how everybody else was making more than they deserved.

We are clearly uncomfortable sharing salary information. By accident, as in this example, or deliberately. But let's ask ourselves: Why? The main reason we cringe when openly sharing compensation is that we fear the reaction of other people. And the main reason they would react badly is if the compensation system is subjective, biased, and unfair. But there is another way.

## The Benefits of the Buffer Zone

The social media marketing company Buffer publishes on its website the formula used to calculate the salary for every position. Variables include the location and skill level of the candidate, from beginner to master.

But Buffer doesn't stop there. It shares a spreadsheet showing the salary of each staff member. Publicly. On its website. At a glance, we can see that the highest-paid employee is the CEO, Joel, who lives in Boulder, Colorado. He earns just under $300,000. The lowest-paid employee is Jess, living in Kalispell, Montana, at $74,000.[1]

According to their employees, there is more accountability and trust as people hold themselves and one another to higher standards. If everyone knows how much I'm making, I had better provide at least that value. Buffer reported a big jump in job applications and a higher retention rate as soon as they went transparent about their salaries.[2]

Full transparency shifts office conversations from speculation and petty jealousy (THEN) to my own skills and contributions (NOW). Instead of "I should make at least as much as Briana," the discussion starts with "Hi, boss. You are classifying me as an intermediate developer. I think I'm a master developer, and here is why."

See how much more productive that conversation is going to be? Both parties start with the same definitions, facts, and understanding of the formula. Paul, for example, can make his case based on his merits instead of petty jealousy about Briana making more. That leads to a negotiation, and even if Paul isn't fully satisfied, at least he has been heard and understands what must happen to reach the next level. That is motivating and encouraging, and it benefits both his career and the company.

If you think full transparency around salaries only works for a hip tech start-up, think again. At Whole Foods, for example, employees can look up the salary of every other employee. In the federal government, the pay for every job is determined by a pay schedule that is publicly available.[3]

## Clap for the Truth

A few years ago, Brené Brown spoke at a global leadership event for Costco in Seattle. She was watching CEO Craig Jelinek take questions from company leaders.

As she explains in her book *Dare to Lead: Brave Work. Tough Conversations. Whole Hearts,*[4] "The questions were tough, but the answers were as tough or tougher. I have seen a lot of CEOs take unvetted questions, and often when the question has a hard answer, the CEO zigzags: 'Great question. Let me give that some thought.' Or 'Wow. Good idea. Let's do some discovery.' But on this cold morning in Seattle there was no zigzagging, only straight talk: 'Yes, we did make that decision and here is why . . .' 'No, we are not going in this direction, and here is how we got to that decision . . .'"

As Brown sat there, she realized, *Damn. I have to go onstage straight after this? The audience will not be friendly.* However, when Jelenik was done, the audience leaped to their feet, clapping and cheering. Shocked, she turned to the woman sitting next to her and said, "That was really hard. He didn't give them the answers they were looking for. Why is everyone cheering?" Her neighbor smiled and said, "At Costco, we clap for the truth." As Brown says: Clear is kind. Unclear is unkind.

We like the truth because, sadly, it is rare. I suspect that your people probably won't regularly give you standing ovations when you tell the hard truth, but I know this: they will appreciate you for telling it as it is. No BS, no pretense. People respect transparency.

## Speak Last

It is well established that the first opinions voiced in a group discussion "anchor" the group in their thinking and heavily influence the ultimate decision. This means the final decision of the group is disproportionally influenced by the first opinion expressed. This is especially true if you as the leader of the group speak first. Simply because of your role as leader, your people will be less likely to offer an alternative view if it conflicts with yours.

Don't be the leader who speaks first. Become a *self-silencing leader*. Let the team share their opinions and debate their views. Fight the urge to jump in. Remember, you already know what you know. What you need to do in meetings is discover what others know that you don't. Facilitate the conversation with questions such as "What are we missing? Who has a different view?" or "What other ideas could we come up with?" When you share your perspective toward the end, you will have the benefit of having heard everybody's opinions without having influenced their thinking.

## NOW Leadership ... NOW!
### *Leaders Speak Last*

At the next team meeting, make a point of letting others go first and speak last. What is the discussion topic you will start with to develop this habit?

I will speak last during the following upcoming team discussion: _____

## May the *Best* Idea Win, Not Necessarily *Yours*

Ray Dalio is the founder of the world's biggest hedge fund firm, Bridgewater Associates, which manages roughly $150 billion. He lives and breathes transparency and has brought the concept into the business mainstream.

As he puts it, "I want independent thinkers who are going to disagree. The most important things I want are meaningful work and meaningful relationships. And I believe that the way to get those is through radical truth and radical transparency. In order to be successful, we have to have independent thinkers ... You have to put your honest thoughts on the table."[5]

Dalio believes transparency encourages better discussions and debate with the ultimate goal of better business outcomes. For example, Dalio's hedge fund records almost every meeting and uses the recordings in company discussions and case studies to evaluate workplace culture. Bridgewater employees also continuously rate colleagues on an app, and all the ratings are accessible in real time by anyone in the company.[6]

Everyone gets rated, including Dalio. In a 2017 TED Talk, he described how a twenty-four-year-old new staffer rated him poorly because he was ill prepared when leading a meeting.[7]

The company's culture is not for everyone, and while Bridgewater got its fair share of criticism for its approach from former employees, some of which have described the company as a "cult,"[8] there is no doubt that Dalio's transparent hedge fund leadership has been immensely successful by its financial performance standards. Since its founding in 1975, it has returned $52.2 billion in gains to its investors—more than any other hedge fund on the planet.

Dalio has also paved the way for others to lead with more transparency. The cryptocurrency firm Coinbase, for example, adopted Bridgewater's employee rating tool on a trial basis in 2022, and Netflix encourages managers to defend controversial decisions, including the choice to fire subordinates, to fellow employees in a process called "sunshining."[9]

We all want our people to buy into our strategy and team goals. This requires that they can freely and openly debate all ideas on the table and feel safe to bring theirs. Most of the leaders I know seek honest discussion and constructive conflict that leads to the best idea winning. Remember: may the *best* idea win, not necessarily *yours* (table 11.1).

Table 11.1: Questions and Insights for Truth Finding[10]

| Question | Insight |
|---|---|
| Do you think more like a soldier or like a scout? | Soldiers defend positions; scout explore new territories. |
| Would you rather be right, or would you rather understand? | Long-term knowledge is way more valuable than short-term wins. |
| Do you seek out opposing views? | Help me understand why you disagree; what does the dissident say? |
| Do you enjoy the pleasant surprise of being mistaken? | Being wrong is a win, not a failure. You just learned something new. |

# NOW Leadership ... NOW!

## *Needing a Knocker*

When discussions in teams start to go in circles or drift off topic, check in on goal consensus and "truth finding" by asking these two questions:

1. Can we review what our objective is right now?
2. Which problem are we trying to solve?

These questions bring the discussion back when it tends to go down a rabbit hole. Encourage and make it safe for all team members to ask these questions. One way to do this is to appoint a "knocker." I often do this when facilitating executive retreats. The job of the knocker is to knock on the table when a discussion goes too far off topic.

## Tell Customers the Truth

Your customers also want and deserve transparency. With growing concerns around food safety, ethical sourcing, data security, and environmental impact, consumers now want to know more about the products they buy than ever before. In fact, in a large-scale study, 86 percent of Americans say transparency from businesses is more important than ever before, and companies are starting to listen.[11]

The Californian online retailer Everlane is transparent about its cost structure. For each product, it publishes a full breakdown on their website of how much it costs to make it, from the price of the raw materials, the manufacturing, and the transportation to exactly how much of a markup Everlane charges customers.[12]

The outdoor apparel company Patagonia is a leader in supply chain transparency. An interactive map on its website offers a glimpse into each cog in Patagonia's extensive list of vendors. Among other things, you can learn how long a factory has worked with Patagonia, the gender ratio, and which items are produced at the facility. On the company's online shopping site, each product contains information about where and how the product is made.

Patagonia truly and authentically cares about the environmental impact of its business operations. Patagonia also understands that to build sticky brands and earn consumers' trust, full transparency is no longer an option—it's a must. Find the full transparency checklist in figure 11.1.[13]

*Figure 11.1: Why Full Transparency? Checklist*

- ✅ Kill the elephant in the room.
- ✅ Unsaid hard things lead to dysfunction and drama.
- ✅ Airing grievances makes addressing and resolving them possible.
- ✅ Team members understand how their work is part of the big picture.
- ✅ Shift from petty jealousy to my own skills and contribution.

- ✅ Saying it as it is builds trust.
- ✅ It leads to more honest and better debates, resulting in better business outcomes.
- ✅ It helps the *best* idea win, not necessarily *yours*.
- ✅ It increases customer loyalty and trust and creates sticky brands.

## Share More by Asking WHY Five Times

You might have heard of the five WHYs, a simple method to determine the root cause of a problem. To get from symptoms to the underlying cause, you simply ask the question WHY five times. The method was developed by Sakichi Toyoda, father of the founder of the Toyota Motor Corporation company, and it was widely used at Toyota during the evolution of its manufacturing methodologies.

Here I am suggesting a different application of the five WHYs. Asking and answering the question five times helps you be open and transparent with yourself and your team about your underlying intentions, reasons, and rationales behind business decisions. It helps you lead with full transparency.

Let's say you just decided to hire a new team member, a brand manager. At the next team meeting, you share and discuss the five WHYs behind that decision.

Your decision: to hire a new brand manager.

1. WHY? Because our workload is going to increase significantly.
2. WHY? Because we are starting a major rebrand push.
3. WHY? Because our current branding is not up to par.
4. WHY? Because we have let our branding efforts slide.
5. WHY? Because we focused on social media outreach and did not make branding enough of a priority.

In five WHYs, you articulated the rationale with clarity. Sharing and discussing the five WHYs makes it easy to be radically transparent about your intentions and goals. As a result, you create buy-in and quite possibly even enthusiasm among team members.

## To Force Honesty, Go First

Eileen Murray, former co-CEO of Bridgewater,[*] took a different approach to force open communication than I did with my team of peacekeepers in Kosovo. Her dilemma: How could she motivate highly talented, headstrong leaders to talk about their anxieties and insecurities?

As Jeffrey Cohn and U. Srinivasa Rangan write in a remarkable piece in *Harvard Business Review*, Murray wasn't willing to let leaders sweep their baggage under the rug. She didn't want tensions or unresolved issues to surface at exactly the wrong time—during a big client presentation, for example. That was too risky for her.

So Murray scheduled regular one-on-one sessions with high-potential leaders—from future CEO candidates to younger, rising stars. She started each of these conversations by sharing her own anxieties and doubts. Murray

---

[*]    Murray left Bridgewater in 2020 under unfriendly terms.

often described what it was like when she first stepped into the office of the CEO as one of the first women to lead a powerful hedge fund.

> You can imagine all of the fears swirling around in my head: fear of looking stupid, fear of getting fired for making a bad decision, fear of saying something that got perversely twisted in the press, fear of letting down my board of directors. I openly shared my angst with subordinates. I was an open book. Honesty is the cornerstone for all trusting relationships, and it had to start with me.[14]

Murray knows that avoiding uncomfortable conversations is counterproductive. These accomplished employees were used to talking about their strengths, but she wanted to talk about the exact opposite: What are your fears? What are your limitations? Why are you sometimes afraid to ask for help?

Because she made these leaders feel safe through her own sharing, they were willing to tackle obstacles in the way of their personal growth and work together to create a leadership development plan.

Murray modeled, insisted, and at times forced open communication about hard topics by leading by example and going first with vulnerability. In the process, she helped some of the best and brightest leaders improve their leadership skills. According to people at Bridgewater, it helped institutionalize a culture of continuous learning.[15]

## Growing Pains

Shifting to full transparency can knock even the toughest leaders around. When you embrace it, be willing to push back and have difficult disagreements that others are not courageous enough to have. It can also be overwhelming when sour opinions come at you from all directions.

Your self-doubt and negative self-talk can fester. You may internalize others' views too much, which can limit your ability to be productive. Transparency can also backfire, at least in the short term, as people often become quieter and more closed off during an onslaught of tough feedback.

Yet this is no excuse not to lead with more transparency. If the COVID-19 crisis taught us one thing, it is that we trust leaders who communicate proactively and with candor. We crave leaders who don't avoid the tough questions. We need leaders who share more and call it as it is.

Here's what it takes to be fully transparent:

1.  Accept that it's not for everybody; you will lose some people along the way. Be OK with that.

2.  Because full transparency can be overwhelming for you, design your own personal safe haven outside of work to recharge (and encourage your people to do the same). This place or activity is where you can be 100 percent yourself and be unconditionally accepted for who you are. My safe places are time spent with my sisters, my mum, my very close friends, and my counselor. I also love my solo time in the mountains.

3.  Make it safe. Full transparency is most effective when people feel safe to speak up, raise doubts, or ask questions without fear of repercussion, being shamed, or worse, risking their career. You need to build a fearless culture based on psychological safety, which, not coincidentally, is our next Shift.

These tensions don't mean full transparency is wrong, and they should not dissuade you from a shift toward it. Rather, I present them to emphasize that you need to be honest about the transition time needed to navigate as people grow accustomed to it and unwavering in your commitment toward this important goal.

The upside is worth it! As a humble leader, you move away from the default of holding your cards close to the vest (THEN) to sharing more (NOW). In the process, you create a healthier, more honest, and more productive team culture. Your people know more about the team's goals and priorities—and care more about each other—which empowers them to execute faster, smarter, and more independently.

# RADICAL HUMILITY

## (THEN) to (NOW)

| What Radical Humility Is Not (THEN) | What Radical Humility Is (NOW) |
|---|---|
| Insecure | Confident |
| Indifferent | Ambitious |
| Wavering | Decisive |
| Hero leader: I know | Learning leader: good at not knowing |
| Individual wins | Team wins |
| I tell | I ask |
| Inflated ego | Accurate view of myself |
| Self-promote | Self-reflect |
| Leadership development is touchy-feely | Leadership is a contact sport |
| I listen to tell | I listen to learn |
| Try to do it all | Focus |
| It's all important | Only a few things really matter |
| Rushed ignorance | Thoughtful deliberation |
| Avoid taking risks | Embrace failure as learning |
| Dwell on failures | Look ahead |
| Fixed mindset | Growth mindset |
| Transactional relationships | Giving a damn about your people |

| What Radical Humility Is Not (THEN) | What Radical Humility Is (NOW) |
| --- | --- |
| Human resources | Seeing each team member as a whole person |
| Build relationships to be "nice" | Build relationships with a business purpose |
| Tear others down | Build others up |
| Deliver tough feedback in a tough way | Deliver tough feedback in a humane way |
| Low standards | High standards |
| Need control | Provide clarity |
| Micromanage | Empower |
| I need to be more involved | I am more relevant |
| Bogged down in details | Provide high-level direction, allocate resources |
| I want the credit | I share the spotlight |
| Tightly hang on to your best people | Embrace losing your best people |
| It's all about me | It's all about the team |
| I am irreplaceable | I make myself obsolete |
| Preserve the perfect façade | Vulnerable learning |
| Blame others | Own your stuff |
| Be right | Get it right |
| Avoidance, secrecy | Transparency |
| HiPPO (highest-paid person's opinion) | Best idea wins |
| I defend my views (soldier) | I improve my views (scout) |
| I confirm my opinion | I seek the truth |

Scan the QR code below for materials that will help you integrate Shift IV: Full Transparency into your daily life:

- reprintable figures
- reprintable tables
- all NOW Leadership . . . NOW prompts from Shift IV consolidated in one place
- bonus content—research, quotes, tool kits, and exercises that will help you toward full transparency

## DIMENSIONS

| | |
|---|---|
| **Self-Knowledge/ Growth Mindset** | SHIFT I<br>**DIG DEEP** |
| **Leading Relationally (Team)/ Growth Mindset** | SHIFT II<br>**TOUGH ON RESULTS, TENDER ON PEOPLE**<br><br>SHIFT III<br>**LEAD LIKE A COMPASS**<br><br>SHIFT IV<br>**FULL TRANSPARENCY** |
| **Leading Relationally (Org.)/ Growth Mindset** | SHIFT V<br>**CHAMPION A FEARLESS CULTURE** |

|   | THEN |   | NOW |
|---|------|---|-----|
|   | Blind spot |   | Self-awareness |
|   | Trying to do it all | → | Laser-sharp focus |
|   | Personal failure as a loss |   | Failing successfully |
|   | Transactional relationships at work | → | Strong personal relationships at work |
|   | Feedback that tears down |   | Feedback that builds up |
|   | Micromanagement | → | Front-line empowerment |
|   | Talent shortage |   | Talent magnet |
|   | False hero, knows-it-all façade | → | Trust through vulnerability |
|   | Avoidance, secrecy |   | Openness, honesty |
|   | Afraid to speak up; hide, cover up mistakes | → | Psychological safety |
|   | Fear-driven culture |   | Fearless culture |

HUMBLE LEADERSHIP = NOW LEADERSHIP

# SHIFT V
# CHAMPION A FEARLESS CULTURE

## Humbly Asking the Big Questions:

1. Why must you champion psychological safety?
2. How do you build a fearless culture/team?

Which would you rather lead?

> **Team #1:** a team of highly talented individuals who are good but not great at working together
>
> OR
>
> **Team #2:** a team of less talented individuals who work great together

I know which I would choose. Give me team #2. Why? Team #2 will outperform team #1 any day!

Despite the very real war for talent, this axiom remains true: culture beats talent. The research on team effectiveness is consistently clear that it matters more how your team works together—the culture—than who is on it. More specifically, what sets high-performing teams apart from the rest is a *fearless culture based on psychological safety* in which team members feel safe to speak up, take risks, make mistakes, and learn.

To be clear, talent still matters. To perform and excel in any endeavor— build electric cars, perform heart surgery, win a major football game—you need skill and expertise. Remember what Jim Collins said about needing the right people on the bus.

Does that mean the more talent, the better? The surprising truth is no. You can have too many stars. Lots of stars means lots of ego. And lots of ego means lots of infighting. Research out of the French Business School INSEAD and Columbia University clearly shows that an NBA basketball team is better off with two stars than four, and a soccer team is better off with three stars than six.[1]

You can have loads of talent and the best plan in the world, but what *really* moves your team from good to great is a fearless culture grounded in psychological safety.

In this Shift, you will learn (1) the case for why, in a world where nonstop learning is required for virtually every job, you must provide a culture of psychological safety for your teams. I will then (2) guide you through the Fearless Team in 4 Steps (FT4S) process to build a fearless culture in your team. This is a culmination of what you've learned throughout this book—and applying it effectively and with urgency is your opportunity to positively impact your teams and organization for many years to come.

# CHAPTER 12
# HAVE YOUR PEOPLE ROCK THE BOAT

*Psychological safety isn't about being nice.*
*It is about giving candid feedback, openly admitting*
*mistakes, and learning from each other.*
**—Prof. Amy Edmondson**[1]

## Why Must You Champion Psychological Safety?

What in the world is *he* doing here?

That was the expression on the faces of the staff sitting in their cubicles as they watched my dad in disbelief as he marched through their offices in his hiking gear, me and my two younger sisters in tow. It was the early 1980s, and my dad had recently been promoted to chief information officer (CIO) of what was then the Swiss national airline, Swissair.

I was thirteen years old. My sisters were eleven and nine. We were on our way back from a hike in eastern Switzerland when my dad decided that he wanted to drop by a remote, small satellite office of his department so he could meet the local staff, well over a hundred kilometers away from headquarters in Zürich.

The manager of the office was five levels below my dad on the organizational chart. The unannounced visit clearly shook her a bit. Anticipating this, my dad brought some local sweet treat to share and break the ice. The manager quickly pushed some chairs together in the conference room and offered coffee for my dad and soft drinks for us kids.

After we sat down, our dad asked to have the rest of the team join us for a few minutes, workload permitting. Most of the team was gathered around the conference-room table. After exchanging some pleasantries, my dad asked about any staff concerns and pain points as a remote office (remember, this was the early 1980s—well before the internet, email, cell phones, and Zoom!). There were some nervous glances as team members were trying to figure out how honest they could be.

My dad doubled down and made it clear that he genuinely wanted to know. "I know you might feel a bit uneasy sharing. This is not about going behind your boss's back. I know that I and my immediate team can always improve and get better, so I really would love to hear your thoughts."

What thirteen-year-old me could not have known at the time was that word had traveled about my dad's leadership style after his promotion to CIO: tough on results but tender on people. So slowly, folks started to open up and talk about what was going well and also what was challenging. I sipped my Coke and paid attention. I remember my dad actively listening and taking notes as the staff shared what was really on their minds. As we were leaving, my dad made a point of shaking everybody's hand, addressing them by their names, and thanking them for their input.

Of course, I did not realize it then, but my dad had helped the team be fearless. By explicitly addressing their potential concerns around sharing, acknowledging that he could do better, inviting input, asking thoughtful questions, actively listening, and offering sincere thank-yous, he had created an environment of psychological safety well before the term was coined. (Between the two chapters of Shift V, I share more about my father's impact on me through his humble leadership.)

## What Is Psychological Safety?

Psychological safety is the shared belief among team members that they are in a safe space for interpersonal risk-taking, with no fear of negative consequences for self-image, status, or career.[2]

Team members understand they will not be rejected or embarrassed for making mistakes or speaking up with their ideas, questions, or concerns. Psychological safety is about being candid, direct, and willing to acknowledge your mistakes by saying, "I screwed up." It is about being willing to be vulnerable and ask for help when you're in over your head, regardless of rank or position.

By providing psychological safety, you enable your team to be fierce. In short, psychological safety lays the groundwork for a fearless culture. And to be clear, psychological safety is *not* about standing around in a circle singing "Kumbaya." It's not about being nice and cozy with one another, and it's most definitely not about lowering performance standards.

If all that sounds familiar, then you're recognizing that at its heart, psychological safety is everything Radical Humility is about for individual leaders, just expanded to an organizational level.

## MBAs versus Kindergarteners

Around 2010 the design engineer Peter Skillman started to hold competitions to find out what makes an outstanding team. He asked four-person teams to build the highest possible structure in eighteen minutes with the following items:

- Twenty pieces of uncooked spaghetti
- One yard of scotch tape
- One yard of string
- One marshmallow

The contest had one rule: The marshmallow has to be on top at the end.

Some of the teams were business school students. The others were kindergarteners.

The timer went off, and the business school students started to strategize right away. They were carefully planning. They discussed their options and came up with smart ideas. They divided their tasks into manageable pieces and kept track of their time.

The kindergarteners did not strategize and did not develop options, ask questions, or plan their time. Instead, they started to build immediately. They were abrupt with one another, even snatching items out of one another's hands. They talked little, but when they talked it was brief and abrupt: "Put it here. Give me this. *No, this.*"[3]

Which teams consistently won?

In dozens of competitions, kindergarteners built structures that were on average more than sixteen inches taller than those of business school students. Kindergarteners also outperformed teams of lawyers by eleven inches and teams of CEOs by six inches.[4]

Why?

Business school students, while seemingly collaborating, were busy managing their power and status. While working on the task, they were distracted by a status question: Who should be in charge? What will they think? How do I not step on their toes? While their interactions appeared professional on the surface, there were lots of inefficiencies below the surface: hesitation, fear of looking stupid in front of the team, subtle jockeying for power. Instead of focusing on the task at hand, they were absorbed in managing their status. In short, they lacked psychological safety.

The kindergarteners, on the other hand, did not care what anybody else thought. They were not afraid to step on toes and didn't compete for status. As the experiment's designer, Peter Skillman, put it, they didn't debate "who should be CEO of Spaghetti Inc."[5] They started to build immediately, took risks, experimented, and offered suggestions. Most of all, they were not afraid to fail.

The kindergarteners did not win because they were more talented or had better skills. They won because they were more skilled at *working together* and having a psychologically safe team.[6]

## The Business Case for Psychological Safety

Google applied the same analytical rigor it applies to its core business when the corporation decided to research what makes a highly effective team.

The widely published 2016 Project Aristotle researched 180 global teams over five years (the most extensive empirical research study to date on team effectiveness) and found that psychological safety—an environment in which team members feel safe speaking up, taking risks, and being vulnerable—was far and away the most important dynamic that set highly productive teams apart from the rest, more important than individual skill set, team size, and tenure.[7]

Google's findings have been replicated in teams in a variety of industries from health care to financial services, confirming that psychological safety is *the* key ingredient to high-quality decision-making, healthy group dynamics, interpersonal relationships, greater innovation, and more effective execution in organizations.[8]

Fear may have once worked as a motivator—certainly in assembly-line days, but even more recently than that. However we now know that cooperation and learning are hindered by fear. Doing our best work is challenging when we feel afraid. Today, highly diverse knowledge and skills are needed to develop a product or provide a service, and as a result, output has become more *team based*. Engineers must seamlessly work with marketers, and salespeople must collaborate with controllers. More stakeholders on the team means more complex projects, and as a result, nonstop learning is demanded for most jobs. A fearless environment has become a must-have for high performance.

As a leader, you are by definition the generalist and rely on your people to proactively communicate with you about their specific areas of expertise. It is therefore imperative that you provide the psychological safety for them to feel comfortable speaking up and coming to you with challenges. It is key for the upstream communication you so clearly rely on to succeed as a leader.

This awareness had been growing among business leaders even before COVID-19 hit. The pandemic accelerated that trend because the higher the ambiguity and need for learning about any given project, the more psychological safety is needed to successfully tackle the project. Many of today's big leadership challenges, from diversity and inclusion to hybrid work and organizational agility, are highly ambiguous and require constant growth and education.

Because a culture of psychological safety is still relatively rare, it can be a true competitive advantage, especially in a post-COVID-19 world. David Murray, CEO of Fortune Media, interviews dozens of Fortune 500 CEOs every year. He found that teams with "strong ties" on average have stayed strong as they faced challenges during the pandemic while teams with "weak ties" have further weakened.[9] Remember the immune system metaphor I shared in chapter 6? This is it in practice.

Strong ties equal high psychological safety cultures, whereas weak ties equal low psychological safety cultures. In short, if your team has a psychologically safe culture where members fearlessly speak up, ask questions, and debate ideas without holding back, you all will get stronger during a crisis, which directly translates to more innovation, speed, engagement, and better bottom-line results.

## Psychological Safety Is Hard and Rare

"I've told my wife that I never plan to fly on it. It's just a safety issue," said Joseph Clayton, a technician at the North Charleston Boeing plant, referring to the Boeing 737 Max in a *New York Times* article. And he was not alone. Following the two deadly 737 Max crashes in 2018 and 2019, internal Boeing emails at the troubled airplane manufacturing plant in South Carolina displayed a pattern of employees complaining to one another with messages like "I'll be shocked if the FAA passes this turd" and "This is a joke. This airplane is ridiculous."[10]

But why wouldn't these Boeing employees speak up about these safety issues to the corporate leaders? The short answer is probably quite obvious to you: a fear of repercussions and a lack of psychological safety. Following the two crashes, Boeing's culture came under intense scrutiny. The evidence revealed a workplace environment dominated by fear, where mechanics and engineers were compelled to adhere to an excessively ambitious production timetable. Employees refrained from voicing concerns, challenging authority, or causing any disruption due to the fear of being the first to lose their jobs. The lack of psychological safety was a major contributing factor to the two deadly crashes.[11]

Boeing is not alone. The scandal at VW over the manipulated diesel engines dubbed "Dieselgate" resulted in a third of VW's market value vanishing overnight. VW had installed illegal software in their diesel vehicle to pass the emissions tests in the lab, but when on the road, the vehicles emitted up to forty times the legally allowed amount.[12] Countless lawsuits, criminal investigations, and incalculable damage to the VW brand can also be traced back to a lack of psychological safety. The culture at VW was such that managers and engineers were threatened with getting fired unless they delivered a clean engine.

Same for the cross-selling scandal at Wells Fargo. The bank opened millions of fraudulent savings and checking accounts on behalf of Wells Fargo's clients without their consent. Wells Fargo employees were pushed to reach highly unrealistic sales targets of opened accounts that were only achievable by cheating, or they were threatened with being let go. Management in effect communicated the message: "You will either find a way to meet the aggressive production schedule (at Boeing), create a clean engine (at VW), or hit the sales target (at Wells Fargo) with the means you have, or we will find someone who can."[13]

These and similar stories have been repeated in organizations large and small across a variety of industries: a top-down, command-and-control leadership approach, highly unrealistic goals, and a culture of fear where people are threatened with firing unless they delivered.[14] When you humbly build a fearless team culture built on psychological safety, you can quite literally save lives.

Despite overwhelming evidence of its benefits, psychological safety is still quite rare. The reasons for this have a lot to do with our human instincts that I touched upon in chapter 4. As humans we want to be liked, we like to please, fit in, and look smart in front of others. It's easy to fulfill some of these needs when we consistently opt to show outward agreement with our boss, even if inwardly we harbor dissent. It's easy to shift blame onto others if it redirects the focus away from our own screwup.

Many well-known sayings were taught to us from our earliest childhood days: "Don't rock the boat" and "If you don't have anything nice to say, don't say anything at all."

Countless studies have shown that humans are deeply loss-averse. Our instincts tell us, "Sure, yeah, learning and personal development are valuable, but I want to avoid situations where I am under the spotlight in front of others, risking potential failures or mistakes." Our natural inclination to seek acceptance and approval often hinders genuine discussions, open sharing of concerns, and the courage to ask hard questions. They have to be prioritized, even when it's difficult.

Harvard professor Amy Edmondson, the leading expert on the subject, demonstrates in her research how hard it is to create psychological safety even in the most straightforward and critical contexts. Someone on a surgical team failing to speak up to avoid cutting on the wrong-side limb occurs because of a fear of speaking up in the medical field, the so-called eminence-over-evidence syndrome. Employees are unwilling to correct the CEO before she shares inaccurate data in a public meeting. Examples like these happen because people are afraid to voice concerns to higher-ups.[15]

## NOW Leadership … NOW!
### *Take the Psychological Safety Quiz with Your Team*

Use these seven questions from Edmondson's *The Fearless Organization: Creating Psychological Safety in the Workplace for Learning, Innovation and Growth*[16] to assess the level of psychological safety in your team. Have your team do the same. Use the results as the basis for a group discussion (1 = strongly agree, 5 = strongly disagree):

1. If you make a mistake on this team, it is often held against you. (R)
2. Members of this team are able to bring up problems and tough issues.

3. People on this team sometimes reject others for being different. (R)
4. It is safe to take risks on this team.
5. It is difficult to ask other members of this team for help. (R)
6. No one on this team would deliberately act in a way that undermines my efforts.
7. Working with members of this team, my unique skills and talents are valued and utilized.

Note that four of the seven items are expressed positively and three expressed negatively (marked with an R). When analyzing the data, you therefore need to "reverse" the score from the negatively worded statements so that 1 becomes a 5, a 2 becomes a 4, and so on.

## Psychological Safety Can Be Achieved

Creating psychological safety is challenging, but it can be done, and ample evidence shows the benefits include better decision-making, more innovation and engagement, and faster and better execution. As a radically humble leader, you know in a Volatile, Uncertain, Complex, and Ambiguous (VUCA) world, you cannot do it all alone. You need your team to feel safe to share their concerns, candidly ask hard questions, and take risks.

In the next chapter, you will learn my Fearless Team in 4 Steps (FT4S) model to build a fearless team culture that is based on psychological safety. Before you start with the four steps, here is one more important point up front: Define the shift you are seeking as a shift to *better results*. Explicitly state to your team the business case for psychological safety covered in this chapter. Be clear that you are not simply attempting to make people feel safe or help them listen better for its own sake. To be sure, these are important things, but they are not the end goal. They are a means to an end—better results for your team.

# RADICAL HUMILITY . . . CLOSE TO HOME

My dad, as I'm sure you can tell from how I speak of him in these pages, was an incredibly influential person in my life. He was also one of the greatest humble leaders I have ever known. This book is in part a tribute to my dad, and I am sharing his story with you because it encapsulates the many ways in which he led with Radical Humility.

His example inspired me to make my own small contribution toward a better world by pursuing military peacekeeping at age fifty. In 1981, when I was fourteen years old, he made what was at the time a highly unconventional decision to take three months of unpaid leave from his highly successful business and academic career to lead a team of relief workers in a refugee camp in Somalia. At age fifty-two, he stepped down from his corporate career and worked in international development and UN election observation assignments in Bhutan, South Africa, Mauritania, Ukraine, and Ghana. He also became a cheesemaker in the Swiss Alps.

My dad passed away in December 2010 at age seventy after a massive stroke in January of that year left him paralyzed and unable to speak, read, or write. He died by assisted suicide, which is legal in Switzerland. At his funeral, I shared my very personal accounts of my dad's life. I thought long and hard about how appropriate and relevant it would be to share my words from that day with you here. Ultimately, I realized my dad's experience wanting to choose how to end his life taught me one of the key lessons of Radical Humility more than a decade ago: the importance of asking big questions without having a clear answer.

- What is a life worth living?
- Who gets to decide?
- How much are pain, suffering, and sacrifice simply part of life?

While what I share from his memorial service is primarily an attempt to share my very own love story with my dad, it touches on important topics that we have covered throughout the book. These lessons are not confined to the workplace:

- Knowing thyself and living a purposeful life, being willing to say no, and remaining true to oneself (Shift I: Dig Deep)
- Combining a demanding, no-nonsense, results-driven leadership approach with warmth, empathy, and understanding (Shift II: Tough on Results, Tender on People)
- Supporting, growing, and loving your kids (and employees!) even when you don't agree with them and knowing when and how to let go (Shift III: Lead Like a Compass)
- Facing your current reality with brutal honesty (Shift IV: Full Transparency)

Dear Papi:

The night before your death, we sat by the fireplace in the house where I grew up with you, Mami, Annette, and Vroni and told you why you are, in so many ways, my life's role model and my best friend. Papi, I know how much you value organization and structure. Therefore, I made an effort to organize my thoughts into three sections.

**First, you were a man of substance who was always true to yourself, often bucking conventions and taking on new challenges.**

Papi, I always admired you for your bold and uncompromising approach to life projects. You critically assessed your professional situation every five years. Unlike the majority of people, you then followed through and made unconventional changes. You had the courage and tenacity to redirect or stop something old and start something new that felt right for you at the time.

One of the most important questions you often asked me when I came to you for advice on a difficult problem was "What feels right to you?" and not "What do others think?" or "How will this or that person perceive this?" And then when I responded "Yes, Papi, it's the right thing for me," that was enough for you. My decision was the right one.

Your example inspired a lot of people, but especially your three children— Annette, Vroni, and me—to pursue our very own passions.

You left this life the same way you lived it: straight as an arrow and without compromising yourself.

### Second, you defined the ideal competitive athlete.

In sports, you pushed yourself hard and leveraged your strict sense of self-discipline.

Much like in your professional career, you were highly demanding of yourself and others in your athletic endeavors.

Papi, we have experienced countless sports adventures together: on cross-country and mountaineering skis, riding our bikes, running, mountaineering, rock climbing, and paddling. Even during the last fifteen years when I was living abroad, we would at least once a year "do something challenging" (as you would say) together.

One memory of our sports adventures has stayed with me in particular. It was in 1991. We were racing a military ski mountaineering competition called the Patrouille des Glacier from Zermatt to Verbier. There were three of us—Major Peter König, Lieutenant Urs König, and Private Köbi Grünenfelder. We'd been at it for thirteen hours, and we were in the last climb up to Rosablanche. Köbi was dog-tired and suggested a quick rest. I was secretly thankful that I did not need to suggest it, but I happily agreed.

However, Papi, although you were fifty-one and more than twice as old as us, you refused to even talk about a rest. I still hear your response as if it were yesterday: "Come on, partners, let's finish it off now!" Then you took off. Köbi and I had no choice but to quietly suffer behind you as we continued the climb toward the finish. Since that time, we turned "Partner, Patrouille des Glaciers" into our secret farewell code, and we used it at many partings at the airports in Zürich, Sydney, and Seattle when one of us was about to walk toward the departure gate.

Papi, before I touch on the third and last point, I want to talk about you as my "über-father." You often told me half-jokingly that you never really were yourself: during the first half of your life, you were merely the "son of the politician father" (your dad was a member of the Swiss National Assembly and a state-level minister), only to then become the "father of the top athlete daughter" during the second half of your life.

You told me that you were told on several occasions, especially during school and your military national service, that as "son of minister König," you had to perform twice as well as anyone else. You also never forgot what your father used to say: "A König boy does not get Cs or Bs but only As." We agreed that your immense drive to perform and to prove yourself was, at least in part, driven by the role your father played in your life.

As a highly driven and competitive person myself, the oldest child and only son of yours, was it sometimes difficult to grow up with a father who was a top-performing athlete and so immensely successful in his academic, business, and personal pursuits? For sure it was. It may even be that my decision to live abroad and establish myself in a world far away from home, despite the intensity and closeness of our relationship, is in part due to the fact that you set virtually unattainable standards here in Switzerland. However, it speaks to the trust between us, as well as our ability to communicate honestly and openly, that you and I were able to talk about this.

Papi, despite this sometimes-difficult dynamic between us, you have remained my Lebensvorbild (life example) and one of my very best friends. The reason for this has to do with my third and final point.

**Third, you were warm, tolerant, and understanding.**

Papi, you were always overscheduled. Your calendar was notoriously overbooked, and you never gave yourself enough unstructured time. However, when one of us needed you or wanted to talk to you, you were always willing to drop all of your well-laid-out plans and be there for us. A lot of people (and not just your immediate family) found you to be a warm, tolerant, honest, and active listener who really cared about all of our professional, family, and relationship issues.

Each of us—your three children—have at times done things in our lives that you did not really approve of. And it always impressed us how you handled that. Your first reaction often was "Urs, Vroni, Annette, is that *really* necessary?" Then we would talk about it, and you would say, "Look, I don't like it and I wouldn't do it, but I love and support you anyway."

Papi, I very much hope that we were able to give you back some of that unconditional warmth, tolerance, and understanding over the span of your life, particularly these last months and weeks of your life. Intellectually, I understand your decision to not want to live in your weakened state anymore. In my heart, however, in my heart—I did not want to let you go.

As painful as it is to not have you with us anymore, you taught me how to deal with an extremely difficult situation like this one. Here it is: "Papi, it hurts. I wish you were still here, but I love you and I support you 100 percent in this decision that feels right to you."

*Partner—Patrouille des Glaciers!*

# CHAPTER 13
# BUILD FEARLESS TEAMS

*Everything you want is on the other side of fear.*
—Jack Canfield

## How Do You Build a Fearless Culture?

Leaving the drab office building and going out into the gray skies of Glogovac, a village of five thousand people in western Kosovo, we are on day two of meetings. My team leader, my observer, and I have just finished talking with two village mayors and are driving to our next meeting with a representative of a local NGO.

As our military SUV turns yet another corner of this constantly winding road, five heavily armed men suddenly jump out of the bushes in front of the vehicle. My team leader slams the brakes, and we swerve left and right before finally coming to a screeching halt. I hear gunfire. My right hand locates the pistol in my holster, but it's too late. The car doors are yanked open, and I am physically forced to the floor while a bag is thrust over my head. One of our attackers takes over the wheel and drives like a maniac while another turns the stereo to full blast.

The whole episode takes all of thirty seconds.

Still trying to get my bearings, my head is still pushed hard against the floor of the SUV by a pistol while my arms are tied behind my back. I am slightly claustrophobic, and having my head covered with a bag makes it hard to breathe, but I do my best not to panic. I try to push the bag up above my chin with my tongue, the only body part I seem to be able to move, but every time the vehicle turns a sharp corner or speeds over a bump, the bag drops again. I find it increasingly difficult to breathe.

I am trying to sense the presence of my teammates. Are they both in the car with me, or was one left behind? I have a sense they are both here, but I'm not sure. Where are they in the SUV? How are they doing?

While worrying about my breathing and my teammates, I suddenly realize that I forgot to do what they taught us during hostage training. To be able to retrace your way back after a potential escape, you are supposed to memorize the route you are driving. How many left turns? How many right turns? In which order? How long in between turns? I realize that I am totally screwed. I have no clue.

Instead, I try to initiate contact with what seems like one of my teammates next to me by gently pushing my knee into whatever body part is there. Again, this is something we have been taught during hostage training. The smallest initiation of body contact like a knee or elbow nudge can provide immense comfort to your fellow hostage. It communicates, hi, I am here, right next to you.

The nudge is reciprocated, and I immediately feel a big relief. We are in this together and will get through it. I respond again with my knee, only for one of our captors (apparently anticipating our actions) to hit it with what seems like the grip of a pistol and yelling, "Head down. Hold still!"

After what seems like a small eternity, the vehicle abruptly stops, and we are yanked outside. I still can't see anything. Two guys start to strip me down. First, off come the boots, and I realize I'm standing in ankle-deep mud. Off comes my weapon, then my uniform top, until I'm in nothing more than my socks and pants.

They tie my feet together, and I get pushed forward into the mud, where I kneel while my hands are tied behind my back. I feel a gun in my back, and I am told not to move, or I'll die. Having no vision and with breathing not getting any easier, I continue trying to create space between my face and the bag with my tongue to make room for more oxygen but without much success. I have no idea where my two teammates are. It becomes quiet, and I still feel the cold gun on my neck. They yell at me numerous times not to move or speak . . . "or else."

Suddenly, I don't feel the gun anymore. It is eerily quiet, and again I wonder where my teammates are. Am I alone? Are they close by? How can I find out? I hear a cough. Could that be a signal? I cough as well. Another cough in response. And right away I feel the gun in my back again. "Don't move!" one man yells again, and he hits me on the shoulders with what seems like a tree branch. What the hell?

After what seems another eternity, I hear the cough again. I respond with a cough and get another one in response. I whisper to find out where my teammates are, all the while worried that our captors are still close by. The potential of the ground being mined adds to the tension. I remember thinking that if we are ever able to free ourselves and take the bags off our heads, we should only step into existing footprints in the mud.

It eventually takes us the better part of an hour, helping each other by using our teeth to get our heads uncovered and our hands and feet free. We have no idea where we are, and we've lost all our equipment and most of our clothing.

What should our next move be?

Now, I must come clean with a full confession . . . this was only a simulation exercise during our military peacekeeping training. We knew it would be coming at some point. However, it still left me more than a little uneasy. I was shaken as it was transpiring, and my team members and I had a lot of work to do to get us out of the mess we were in. It wasn't real, but we really did have to collaborate to get free and get home.

This learning experience of living through an assault made us grow immensely as a team. We had to work together through a highly stressful situation. We experienced one another helpless and vulnerable, and we had to rely on one another. We literally were helping one another out of the mud, taking calculated risks, making mistakes, correcting them, and following the lead of whoever was ready and able to take it at the time, regardless of rank.

During the after-action review (AAR), we discussed and acknowledged the mistakes we made individually and as a team. I made a point of taking responsibility for my difficulty to do much beyond taking care of myself while I was fighting my slight claustrophobia and not remembering the route we drove. Owning my mistake in turn made it safe for my teammates to own their errors.

As a result of going through this stressful learning experience and a meaningful and honest AAR, we deepened our relationships. Our bond and trust grew immensely, and we moved our team one step closer toward a fearless culture.

## A Fearless Team in 4 Steps (FT4S)

How do you create psychological safety so you can build a fearless team?

It's your turn now!

Take your team through the Fearless Team in 4 Steps (FT4S) shown in figure 13.1. If the steps in this tool look familiar, it's because we've discovered the importance of and learned how to apply all four of these steps at various stages of the book so far. The FT4S is the culmination of your learning.

1. Reframe failure.
2. Encourage speaking up.
3. Acknowledge and thank.
4. Train psychological safety by experientially learning together.

*Figure 13.1: A Fearless Team in 4 Steps (FT4S)*

## 1. Reframe Failure

In chapter 5, I showed you how to fail successfully on an individual level when I illustrated the steps that helped me to follow up my near-death experience and the biggest athletic failure of my life with the best ultracycling season of my career. Here, I will focus on how you must reframe failure for your team. Because fear of failure is such a clear indicator of low psychological safety, you must reframe failure as an opportunity to grow and learn versus something to be ashamed of or cover up.

Reframing failure does not mean, of course, that we like failing any more than before, but it does mean that you make it clear that each failure will be treated as an opportunity to learn and grow.

## NOW Leadership ... NOW!
### *Whoops-a-Daisy*

From Kim Scott's previously mentioned book *Radical Candor*, here is a low-tech, cheap method to encourage praise and normalize failure with two stuffed animals, a whale and a flower. At the next team meeting, invite your people to nominate someone for the Killer Whale award. The idea is to have team members talk about some outstanding work they have seen somebody else do. The winner each week gets to decide who deserves to win the following week. Then people self-nominate for the Whoops-a-Daisy. If somebody messed up, they stand up and share what happened. This can help somebody else avoid making the same mistake, and it's also a powerful exercise to help normalize the acknowledgment of mistakes.[1]

I will introduce the Killer Whale and the Whoops-a-Daisy to my team on: _____

Not all failures are equal, of course, and different failures require a different response from you as the leader (see table 13.1). Edmondson distinguishes between preventable failures (never good news), complex failures (still not good news), and intelligent failures (not fun but must be considered good news because of the value they bring to learning and innovation).[2]

When a failure occurs because someone purposely took an illegal shortcut (preventable failure), your response needs to be disciplinary action. If one of your assembly-line workers forgets to wear their safety gear (also a preventable failure), you might need to deal with it by providing additional training or improving the existing processes. On the other hand, the approach to handling a complex failure, like a surgical procedure not achieving the desired outcome, must be different again.

With complex failures, you want to conduct a thorough AAR and identify risk factors to prevent the failure in the future. My Race Across America failure I shared in chapter 5 falls into this category. My sodium overload combined with the altitude were complex and novel factors imposed on a familiar situation (my long-distance racing).

Your response to a well-designed prototype not working out the way you had hoped (intelligent failure) might actually be worth a failure party because of all the valuable lessons learned.

Whether failures are good news or not, you must make it explicit for your people that failure will sometimes happen. Everybody should feel safe enough to "say something when they see something."

After you have reframed failure for your team, it is time to invite and ask for active participation and take steps to encourage your team members to speak up.

*Table 13.1: Three Types of Failure:*
*Causes and Productive Leadership Response[3]*

| | Preventable | Complex | Intelligent |
|---|---|---|---|
| **Definition** | Process deviation: not following well-known processes | System breakdown: unique and new combination of events | Failed trial: venture into the unknown |
| **Examples** | Assembly line<br><br>Fast-food service | Hospitals<br><br>Aircraft | New product development<br><br>Research |
| **Causes** | Behavior, skill, and attention deficiencies | Complex and novel factors imposed on familiar situations | Great uncertainty, trial and error, risk-taking |
| **Failure Celebration** | Celebrate those who notice small deviation from process early as observant. "Good catch celebration" | Combination "Good catch celebration" for preventable and "Failure Party" for intelligent | Celebrate failure as an integral part of learning and innovation, i.e., "Failure Party" |
| **Productive Leadership Responses** | Training<br><br>System and process and system improvement<br><br>Disciplinary action if repeated or bad-faith failure | AAR: failure analysis from different perspective<br><br>Identify risk factors<br><br>System improvement | Failure awards<br><br>Analysis of outcome<br><br>Brainstorm new hypothesis<br><br>Design next experiment |

## 2. Encourage Speaking Up

Alan Mulally, best known for his impressive turnaround of the Ford Motor Company, writes in the book *The Extraordinary Power of Leader Humility: Thriving Organizations, Great Results* that during his first few weeks at Ford, in senior leadership meetings all business dashboard indicators were on green, meaning "on plan" (versus yellow, meaning "not on plan but have a process to get back on plan," or red, "not on plan and need help"). He of course knew this could not be true, so he said, "You know, we are losing billions of dollars. Isn't there anything that is not going well?"

It took some time, but the first person to speak up was Mark Fields (who succeeded Mulally as CEO at Ford). Fields announced that Ford would hold off the launch of the highly anticipated Edge car.[4]

In the book *American Icon: Alan Mulally and the Fight to Save Ford Motor Company*, Bryce Hoffman describes the scene when Mark Fields reported the hold on the Ford Edge: "And on the Edge launch, we're red. You can see it there," he said, pointing at the screen. "We're holding the launch." Everyone turned toward Fields. So did Mulally, who was sitting next to him.

*Dead man walking*, thought some peers. Suddenly, someone started clapping. It was Mulally. "Mark, this is great visibility," he beamed. "Who can help Mark with this?"[5] It took another few meetings with mainly green lights and people observing how Mulally reacted. Was he criticizing Fields? Was he firing him? No. Instead, he applauded Fields for his guts to speak up, and after a few weeks more, people were willing to share yellow and red lights. The team could finally get to work successfully turning the Ford Motor Company around. Instead of shooting the messenger, Mulally was hugging the messenger.

Mulally is a fantastic example of how to encourage your people to speak up. This practice means humbly acknowledging your own gaps in knowledge, asking powerful questions, and listening with intent with the overarching goal of making it safe for your team members to speak up about bad news or when they disagree with you.

One pushback I sometimes hear from leaders is this: I have some team members who already are taking up too much of the air in the room. You want me to encourage them to talk even more? My comeback is this: I hear you. Many of us have a team member who enjoys the sound of their own voice a bit too much. But here is the important distinction: speaking up fearlessly about important topics and droning on are not the same thing. I bet the person on your team who talks too much would also like to be more successful in their job. If shutting up would help that person become a more effective employee, then it is your job to deliver that feedback—but that's about performance, not psychological safety.

### Humbly Own Your Gaps

If everyone feels that the boss has all the answers and always needs to have the last word, no one will speak up. Don't be that boss. Acknowledge your gaps. You might tell your people, "I am really not sure about this and would like your input. What am I not seeing?" or "Everybody has blind spots. I do too. I want you to tell me where you disagree with me."

When you ask powerful questions and practice active listening, you are building a fearless culture. It's that simple! Powerful questions are most often open-ended questions that come from a place of wanting to learn (as opposed to judging, for example). By asking powerful questions, you are telling your people that you are genuinely interested in their point of view.

Make it clear that the team needs everyone speaking up with candor so that together you all can achieve success. Say things like "I need to hear from everyone" or "Who have we not heard from?"

When thinking about what makes a powerful question, consider these three examples:

"How much do you need to exercise each week?"

*versus*

"What would 'being fit' look like for you?"

"Is there more to be learned here?"

*versus*

"How can you double the learning from this experience?"

"What are the training options available?"

*versus*

"What do you want to know that you don't know today?"

See how the second question in all three pairs is much more thought-provoking ("double the learning"), aims at exposing underlying assumptions ("what would fit look like?"), and creates new possibilities ("what do you want to know that you don't know today").

See table 13.2 for a list of what makes a powerful question, with some strong examples for each category.

*Table 13.2: What Makes for a Powerful Question?*

| | Criteria | Examples |
|---|---|---|
| ✅ | Is open-ended (can't be answered with "Yes" or "No") | What/How/When/ (Why) questions |
| ✅ | Is thought provoking | "What will we know a year from now that we do not know now?" <br><br> "What are we missing here?" <br><br> "What if . . . ?" <br><br> "What might be our competitor's next move?" |
| ✅ | Helps create new possibilities | "What is the moonshot option here?" <br><br> "If we had nothing to lose, what would we do?" |
| ✅ | Exposes underlying assumptions | "What are we not seeing?" <br><br> "What are we assuming?" <br><br> "How can we reframe this problem?" |
| ✅ | Comes from a place of curiosity, not judgment ("Why" questions, while powerful, can come across as judgmental: "Why did you do this?") | "Help me understand how . . ." <br><br> "What are you hearing from our customers?" |
| ✅ | Focuses attention | "What is our most important goal?" <br><br> "What are the three things we can do right now to achieve our number one goal?" |

| | Criteria | Examples |
|---|---|---|
| ✓ | Builds on the other person's exploration | "How come this is important to you?"<br><br>"Keep going; say more." |
| ✓ | Reframes a problem | "How else might we look at this?"<br><br>"What's another lens to look at this through?" |
| ✓ | Generates more powerful questions | "What are we not thinking about?"<br><br>"What would Albert Einstein / Madame Curie / Warren Buffett / Mother Teresa . . . (fill in a genius in your industry) want to know?"<br><br>What if . . . ? |

# NOW Leadership . . . NOW!

## Start Inquiring

Pick your one or two favorite questions from table 13.2 and start asking them in your next team meeting or one-on-one.

The question I will ask is: _____.

*Bonus:* Withstand the silence after you ask a question. Don't just fill it because it feels uncomfortable. A great rule of thumb is to count slowly to five in your head. Don't let your partner off the hook. People won't wait that long and will respond. Let the silence do the heavy lifting.

For many of us, the prevailing mode of listening is still to merely look to respond and show off how smart we are by telling what we know or to advance our own agenda. As our teams are becoming increasingly diverse with many different points of view represented, *really* listening has become more important than ever.

The willingness to truly listen to what others are saying requires discipline, but it can be learned. The three levels of listening first developed by the Co-Active Training Institute, which I teach in my coaching workshops, are a useful framework to help you up your listening game. Your goal is to elevate your listening to Level 3.[6]

*Level 1: Internal Listening (Self Focused)*
At this level, you are focused on yourself and how what you are hearing affects you. You may be thinking, "I've had the same experience" or "What should I say now?" At Level 1, you have your agenda and are therefore often only half-hearing what the other person is saying. Most of our listening happens at Level 1.

*Level 2: Focused Listening (Other Focused)*
At this level, you are deeply focused on the other person and their thoughts and feelings. This is deep, active listening. When you listen at Level 2, you might be thinking, "This issue must be very important to her." Listening at Level 2 helps you to better understand someone else's motivations and perspectives. Level 2 listening takes a conscious effort. It requires you to be truly present in the moment.

*Level 3: Global Listening (Context Focused)*
Level 3 is the high art of listening. You not only hear what is said, but you are tuned into *what is not said*. When you listen at Level 3, you pick up on the energy of the conversation and notice changes in body language and tone of voice. These energetic shifts are often subtle, so as a listener you must be 100 percent present to be able

to pick up on them. If Level 2 is laser-sharp, focused listening, then Level 3 is broadening out, contextual listening, paying attention to every component of the conversation.

By upping your listening game to Level 3 and truly hearing and seeing your people, you take an important step in creating a fearless culture.

## NOW Leadership ... NOW!
### *Elevating Your Listening*

During your next interaction with a team member, practice Level 2 and Level 3 listening.

*Practice Level 2 listening:* Take a few deep breaths before going into a conversation. Center yourself. Immerse yourself in the moment, forget what was happening before and what will come after, and give the other person your full attention. When you notice your mind wandering to Level 1 listening (and it will!), simply let those thoughts go and return to Level 2.

The person I will practice Level 2 listening with is _____

*Practice Level 3 listening:* Zoom out. As the other person is speaking, notice their tone of voice, body language, and energy level. Do they seem exhausted, hesitant, excited, unsure, frustrated? If you feel comfortable, you might ask, "I noticed you paused before saying that. Is there anything about this decision that gives you pause?" Or "I sense you have a lot of energy around this topic. Do I read that right?"

The person I will practice Level 3 listening with is _____

### 3. Acknowledge and Thank

Acknowledging and thanking is simple, but it's not easy. It can be hard to be thankful for a contribution that challenges your own beliefs, yet it is so important to do it. Even if you disagree with the point that is brought to you, your job is to acknowledge and thank. If you don't—or even worse, if you discount or belittle the input—you can be sure that next time around, nobody will speak up. As discussed in chapter 11, you need the *best* idea to win, not *your* idea.

Remember from chapter 3: You always ask, you always listen, you always thank, but as the leader, you get to decide. Whether the suggestion or idea brought to you is good or bad, your initial response always needs to be "Thank you for bringing this up." That sentence alone increases psychological safety. Doing it publicly is even more powerful. When you thank your people for disagreeing with you in public, you encourage others to speak up as well. Most of all, you are modeling the behavior you want to see in your people.

After you've taken your team through these three steps of (1) reframing failure, (2) encouraging speaking up, and (3) acknowledging and thanking, it is time for Step 4 of Fearless Team in 4 Steps (FT4S)—to train and reinforce a fearless culture in your team by experientially learning together.

## 4. Experientially Learn Together

One of the most effective and powerful ways for you as a humble leader to transform your team into a high-performing unit is to have your team members experientially learn together—much like my team did during hostage training. Training that is experiential is remembered more vividly and for a longer time. I speak from experience.

The key ingredient must be the vulnerable process of *learning* (which of course includes failing) for all. Importantly, you as the leader must model—publicly—your processes of learning and failing. The concept of the leader as role model must evolve from the supposedly perfect hero leader (THEN) to the work-in-progress leader who is high on Radical Humility and a willingness to learn and grow but low on thinking they have all the answers (NOW).[7] Remember chapter 2?

When you set this example as a leader, you send a strong signal to all your team members that it is safe to be practicing, failing, and developing. I, for one, had to learn that even though I was the commander of the team,

I was not able to provide meaningful guidance to my team members while I was fighting my slight claustrophobia. At that moment I was more than happy to vulnerably let my observer and team leader guide my actions. In the process, I helped to build a fearless team.

As part of my ongoing training as a military peacekeeper, I had the "pleasure" of undergoing sometimes-lengthy hostage simulations numerous times after this initial training. The experience itself sucked every time, but without fail my team gained the same bonding, expanded trust, and increased psychological safety after having supported one another through the highly stressful experience.

## Proof That You Can Create a Fearless Culture

You don't have to take your team members hostage (HR will take issue!), but there are plenty of examples in the business world that demonstrate the value of experientially learning together to craft a fearless culture.

Here are just a few. As you read through these, think about what experiential training you may be able to create with your team to shift to a fearless culture.

### Cooking and Eating Together

We are often searching for that silver-bullet solution that will help us build a high-performing team, but a solution might be much simpler than we think. Though it's often overlooked, cooking and eating together as a team can foster psychological safety. Studies with teams of firefighters and surgical teams in hospitals have shown that teams perform significantly better on the job when they cook and eat together. The *experiential learnings* that underlie simple meal planning—communication and collaboration—show up in work actions.[8]

A similar effect was observed by researchers in the call centers of Bank of America, where employees deal with notoriously low morale and high stress. By simply syncing the coffee break to the same fifteen minutes for everybody, buying nicer coffee machines, and replacing four-person tables with ten-person tables, they were able to increase productivity by 20 percent and reduce turnover from 40 to 12 percent.[9]

### Working the Floor at Taco Bell

Taco Bell has a slightly unorthodox but highly effective way of onboarding new corporate employees. Each one must work at one of the fast-food chain's restaurants for a week of *experiential learning*. In addition to the weeklong training when they start, corporate employees are required to complete a full shift at a store each year. They take orders from customers, work the food prep lines, and handle cleaning and closing responsibilities.

Taco Bell CEO Mark King, who also worked a crew shift during onboarding, says he's a better leader as a result. The hands-on training is an important, humbling experience that levels the hierarchy and ensures frontline employees feel safe to speak up and bring issues to the attention of corporate.[10]

### Learning Together in Japan

Dr. Gary Kaplan, the now-retired CEO of the Virginia Mason Hospital System in Seattle, was the first health-care leader to successfully implement the Toyota Lean method in health care in the early 2000s. Looking back, Dr. Kaplan reflects that one of the key factors of success was taking his executive team and the board to Japan to *experientially learn the Toyota method together.* "By going on these trips and learning together, they formed strong relationships that made the board an essential support system for the change initiative."[11]

The massive change initiative Kaplan spearheaded at Virginia Mason transformed the organization into a more resilient health-care giant grounded in a fearless culture. But it would have most likely failed miserably if it weren't for the shared learning experience of these regular trips to Japan, starting at the very top with the board.

### *Fearless through* Les Misérables

Once per year the entire staff at Front, a workflow application business, puts on a musical. Recently it was *Les Misérables* with the CEO and founder as Cozette. Creating and practicing a musical together creates an environment where people can and need to be vulnerable, take risks, make mistakes, fail, try again, fail again, and finally improve. *That* is experiential learning.

Whether they're dancing, singing, narrating, or playing an instrument, it brings the team together. And the track record of the Front teams speaks for itself: acquiring more than seven thousand customers, raising almost $140 million in funding, and closing the books on its first acquisition.[12]

These examples may not fit your specific situation, but I hope they provide some inspiration for you. Now, how will you create experiential learning experiences for your team to help create and train a fearless culture where everyone's voice is heard and your team members feel free to speak up?

## NOW Leadership ... NOW!
### *Cook and Eat with Your Team*

Schedule a team-building activity that involves cooking together. Whether off-site at a culinary school or a chef-hosted event in your office, get your people to plan, prepare, and enjoy a meal together. We will cook and eat together on: _____

Alternatively, and very easy to set up: Encourage your team to eat meals together by simply scheduling team lunches on the calendar, setting the expectation so your team can plan ahead.

## Be a Watchdog

Building a fearless team culture takes time and energy, but it can vanish in mere moments.

It is your job as champion of a fearless culture to avoid that at all costs, which means you have to be a watchdog that encourages actions and words that promote openness and push back against even seemingly small acts of disrespect or rudeness. Eye-rolling or interrupting can push a team back into a fear-based culture. Be vigilant, speak up firmly, and correct when you notice your team members slipping.

*Table 13.3: The Watchdog's DOs and DON'Ts List for a Fearless Team Culture*

| DON'T | DO |
|---|---|
| Eye roll, smirk, sneer | Use respectful body language |
| Interrupt | Let others finish their point |
| Stonewall | Engage with others |
| Meeting after the meeting | Say all you have to say in the meeting |
| Use hostile humor at the expense of others | Use good-natured, self-deprecating humor |
| Mock, mimic, use sarcasm | Speak firmly but with respect |
| Act like a know-it-all | Humbly own your gaps |
| Ask to judge | Ask to learn |
| Listen to respond | Listen to understand |
| Condescend | Speak eye to eye: we are in this together |

## NOW Leadership ... NOW
### *Watchdog Training*

Observe your team's interaction for a week using table 13.3 as a guide and jot down what you see. Share your observations with your team and set the expectation that going forward you will be the watchdog for a culture of psychological safety, reenforcing the dos and correcting the don'ts immediately and in the moment.

I will start collecting my observations on: _____

## All Eyes Are on You
## (But It Doesn't Mean It's All about You)

Despite increasing evidence and personal examples, fearless teams are still rather rare. Old habits die hard. This is exactly why developing a fearless culture can be a competitive advantage for your organization.

Our world continues to be a volatile place. The need for speaking up about important issues facing your team will only increase. In time, a fearless culture won't be the exception but rather the ante to work for any successful team or organization. Be a catalyst for that change!

As you've now learned, championing a fearless culture is not easy, but it can be done. Be encouraged that despite inevitable setbacks and mistakes, you can and will make progress if you follow the FT4S model. Know that by championing psychological safety in your team, you are steadily moving toward a fearless culture. Start your fearless journey today. Embrace the struggles and celebrate the wins. And always remember that growth lies behind door number discomfort.

My last piece of advice to you is simply this (and after having read these pages, this will not come as a surprise to you):

Lead by example.

I am sure you've experienced bosses who demand speaking up with candor about your mistakes and then fail to demonstrate it themselves. Talk is cheap, and action is where it's at when it comes to psychological safety. All eyes are on you, always (but it doesn't mean it's all about you). As a leader you are always onstage, and your people observe your every move—what you do and don't do, what you say and don't say. The show is always on.

Model the behaviors you are asking for, publicly acknowledge mistakes, share your shortcomings, and show genuine interest in what your people have to say. Practice this, and you will be well on your way to transforming your team into a fierce and fearless unit. There is no stopping a team like that. It's what the world needs now.

Commit (NOW) to lead with Radical Humility!

# RADICAL HUMILITY

## (THEN) to (NOW)

| What Radical Humility Is Not (THEN) | What Radical Humility Is (NOW) |
| --- | --- |
| Insecure | Confident |
| Indifferent | Ambitious |
| Wavering | Decisive |
| Hero leader: I know | Learning leader: good at not knowing |
| Individual wins | Team wins |
| I tell | I ask |
| Inflated ego | Accurate view of myself |
| Self-promote | Self-reflect |
| Leadership development is touchy-feely | Leadership is a contact sport |
| I listen to tell | I listen to learn |
| Try to do it all | Focus |
| It's all important | Only a few things really matter |
| Rushed ignorance | Thoughtful deliberation |
| Avoid taking risks | Embrace failure as learning |
| Dwell on failures | Look ahead |
| Fixed mindset | Growth mindset |
| Transactional relationships | Giving a damn about your people |

| What Radical Humility Is Not (THEN) | What Radical Humility Is (NOW) |
|---|---|
| Human resources | See each team member as a whole person |
| Build relationships to be "nice" | Build relationships with a business purpose |
| Tear others down | Build others up |
| Deliver tough feedback in a tough way | Deliver tough feedback in a humane way |
| Low standards | High standards |
| Need control | Provide clarity |
| Micromanage | Empower |
| I need to be more involved | I am more relevant |
| Bogged down in details | Provide high-level direction, allocate resources |
| I want the credit | I share the spotlight |
| Tightly hang on to your best people | Embrace losing your best people |
| It's all about me | It's all about the team |
| I am irreplaceable | I make myself obsolete |
| Preserving the perfect façade | Vulnerable learning |
| Blame others | Own your stuff |
| Be right | Get it right |
| Avoidance, secrecy | Transparency |
| HiPPO (highest-paid person's opinion) | Best idea wins |
| I defend my views (soldier) | I improve my views (scout) |
| I confirm my opinion | I seek the truth |
| Fear of repercussions for speaking up | Feel safe to voice my opinion |
| Excel at individual leadership skills | Own the culture of my team |

| What Radical Humility Is Not (THEN) | What Radical Humility Is (NOW) |
| --- | --- |
| Fear, anxiety | Psychological safety |
| Respond equally to all failures | Vary response to different kind of failures |
| Sweep failures under the carpet | Reframe failure as growth opportunity |
| Listen to confirm | Listen to learn |
| Shoot the messenger | Hug the messenger |
| Role model = perfect hero leader | Role model = humble learning leader |
| Classroom training | Experientially learn together |

Scan the QR code below to print your very own poster of the figure of what Radical Humility is (NOW) and what it is not (THEN) that we have been building throughout this book.

Scan the QR code below for materials that will help you integrate Shift V: Champion a Fearless Culture into your daily life:

- reprintable figures
- reprintable tables
- all NOW Leadership . . . NOW prompts from Shift V consolidated in one place
- bonus content—research, quotes, tool kits, and exercises that will help you champion a fearless culture

# YOUR CALL TO ACTION

*Nothing changes if nothing changes.*
—**A frequently used mantra in recovery groups**

## How Will You Practice NOW Leadership . . . NOW?

"Thank you, Captain, for being here, and thank for driving the Serbs out. They raped and killed our wives and children. Without you here, they would be right back. Thank you, Captain."

These were the words of the mayor of the town I was stationed in as we shook hands across the coffee table, saying our goodbye and wrapping up our final meeting before the end of my tour in Kosovo.

Unlike many politicians in Kosovo, the mayor was a decent man, and I knew he was right about the atrocities that happened (although it should be noted, to some extent these occurred on both sides). As he shook my hand, I felt yet again a deep sense of humility. His very personal words made me realize how hard it still is for me to truly appreciate how much pain, suffering, resentment, and mistrust there is in Kosovo on this very long, winding road to peace.

At the end of 2017, I returned to my boys, my home, my friends, and my business a much humbler person—a humbler dad, a humbler peacekeeping officer, and indeed a much humbler leader. Sometimes it felt the more I learned, the less I seemed to know, and the more I studied, the less I seemed to understand. But the quality of my questions improved, and that's no small feat.

Instead of asking myself (remember?), "How can I ensure I never, ever drop this damn flak jacket ever again?" I was pondering, "Is our peacekeeping force a crutch?" Are we keeping the people in Kosovo from truly taking their young nation's destiny into their own hands?

I was asking better and harder questions about bigger topics.

As a (NOW) leader, I implore you to do the same:

- How can you dig deep to truly get to know thyself? (Shift I)?
- How can you develop and deepen relationships that increase productivity *and* connection? (Shift II)
- How do you park your ego at the door and let your teams shine? (Shift III)
- How can you build trust by sharing more of yourself? (Shift IV)
- How can you get more comfortable with ambiguity and failure (it's part of the job description these days)? (Shift V)

As you now know, this is what Radical Humility is all about—not just in military peacekeeping but in business, leadership, and life.

And yet—and yet!—gaining new insights by asking big questions is not enough. The opening quote reminds us that our life is ultimately shaped by the small decisions we make every day and that we need to follow up learning with action in the real world.

By reading this book, you now have the knowledge and practical hands-on tools to become a badass leader by practicing Radical Humility. Let the 5 THEN to NOW Leadership Shifts displayed in their entirety in the final figure be your guidepost. Take inspiration from the leadership stories I shared. Most importantly, apply your learnings through the NOW Leadership . . . NOW prompts.

*The 5 THEN to NOW Shifts to Radical Humility*

| DIMENSIONS | | THEN | NOW | |
|---|---|---|---|---|
| Self-Knowledge/ Growth Mindset | SHIFT I DIG DEEP | Blind spot / Trying to do it all / Personal failure as a loss | Self-awareness / Laser-sharp focus / Failing successfully | |
| Leading Relationally (Team)/ Growth Mindset | SHIFT II TOUGH ON RESULTS, TENDER ON PEOPLE | Transactional relationships at work / Feedback that tears down | Strong personal relationships at work / Feedback that builds up | |
| | SHIFT III LEAD LIKE A COMPASS | Micromanagement / Talent shortage | Front-line empowerment / Talent magnet | HUMBLE LEADERSHIP = NOW LEADERSHIP |
| | SHIFT IV FULL TRANSPARENCY | False hero, knows-it-all façade / Avoidance, secrecy | Trust through vulnerability / Openness, honesty | |
| Leading Relationally (Org.)/ Growth Mindset | SHIFT V CHAMPION A FEARLESS CULTURE | Afraid to speak up; hide, cover up mistakes / Fear-driven culture | Psychological safety / Fearless culture | |

So, I ask you: What is the difference you will make? What actions will you take? It's your time (NOW)! I leave you with one final prompt:

## NOW Leadership ... NOW!

The one action I will take as a leader invested in Radical Humility after putting this book down is _____

_____

To access and print all the NOW Leadership . . . NOW! prompts and all opening quotes, scan the below QR code.

Scan the QR code below for materials that will help you integrate Radical Humility into your daily life, including:

- A monthly newsletter
- Additional tips on how to lead

# ACKNOWLEDGMENTS

Writing this book has been the ultimate humbling experience, and I am deeply grateful to the many individuals who have contributed their time, expertise, support, and love to bring it to life.

First, I would like to express my heartfelt appreciation to the colleagues and friends who generously reviewed earlier drafts and provided invaluable feedback: Colin Bryar, Courtney Hughes, Ivana Lichtscheidl, Jennifer Duncan, Josh Wymore, Ken Barnes, Lauren Owen, Patti Hawkins, Peter Polson, Santor Nishizaki, and Shannon Huffman Polson—you took time out of your busy lives to dive deep into the manuscript. Your insightful suggestions and constructive criticism have elevated the quality of this work.

A special shout-out goes to Conner Krizancic. You not only provided highly relevant feedback on the manuscript, but you continue to be a damn pleasure to work with as my go-to digital native who helps me spread my message. You will go far.

I am immensely grateful to Joanne Gordon, writer extraordinaire, whose expertise has been instrumental in refining the structure and through line of this book. Your contributions have added great clarity to my message. I am honored you took time away from your busy book projects to help me improve my work.

Kudos go to Nick Lucht, whose thorough fact-checking has ensured the integrity of the information presented in these pages.

The help of all these people, from development to line editing, is humbling. Any errors in the final version of this book are mine and mine alone.

My writing coach, Myles Schrag, has been with me along the whole journey from first outline to final manuscript. Your professional and empathetic coaching as well as your expertise and willingness to sift through countless rounds of reviews are second to none. I could not have asked for a better guide. There is no doubt that this book would never have made it without you. A heartfelt thank-you.

To the team at Amplify Publishing Group, Naren Aryal and Brandon Coward, I extend my gratitude for your belief in this project and for your support throughout the sometimes mysterious publishing process.

A heartfelt thank-you goes to the ImpactEleven team, especially Josh Linkner, Seth Mattison, Connor Trombley, and Jordan Broad. You helped relaunch me on my speaking journey, and for that I am grateful. I humbly look forward to continuing to learn from your remarkable work.

I would like to express my sincere appreciation to my leadership clients over the years. Thank you for your trust, vulnerability, and willingness to do the hard work and transform into the very best leaders you can be. Your growth and learning have given my work purpose.

Thank you to my competitors and friends in the ultraendurance scene for the intense and exhilarating experiences over the years on snow, on foot, and on the bike. There are too many of you to list here. You know who you are. Thank you for being tough as nails on the course and laid-back and friendly off it.

I want to acknowledge my brothers and sisters in arms who serve in peacekeeping missions worldwide. Our work is not perfect, yet our cause remains noble. Thank you for your selflessness and dedication to protecting the most vulnerable and preserving peace and security around the globe.

A loving thank-you to my sisters and mum. Mami, Vroni, and Annette, you provide me with unconditional love and support through the inevitable ups and downs of life. Despite our geographic distance over the past thirty years, our family bond has become even stronger. For that, I am immensely grateful.

And finally, to the two most important men in my life—my two sons, Luc and Liam. I know how hard my peacekeeping work is on you. Thank you for keeping our connection and love going strong even when I am many miles away. Throughout my missions, you've shown maturity beyond your years. I am immensely proud of the thoughtful, engaged, compassionate, and humble young men you have become.

# ENDNOTES

## Introduction

1    KFOR SWISSCOY. "KFOR SWISSCOY," n.d. https://www.vtg.admin.ch/en/
news/einsaetze-und-operationen/militaerische-friedensfoerderung/missionen/
swisscoy.html; "NATO Mission in Kosovo (KFOR)," n.d. https://shape.nato.int/
ongoingoperations/nato-mission-in-kosovo-kfor-.aspx; Kosovo War - Wikipedia.
"Kosovo War - Wikipedia," September 1, 2009. https://en.wikipedia.org/wiki/
Kosovo_War.

## Chapter 1

1    These works by practitioners are a good starting point:

> Everett L. Worthington Jr., Don E. Davis, and Joshua N. Hook, ed.,
> *Handbook of Humility: Theory, Research and Applications* (New York:
> Routledge, 2017).

> Amer Kaissi, *Humbitious: The Power of Low-Ego, High-Drive Leadership*
> (Vancouver: Page Two Press, 2021).

> Edgar A. Schein and Peter A. Schein, *Humble Leadership: The Power of
> Relationships, Openness, and Trust* (Oakland: Berrett-Koehler, 2018).

> Edward D. Hess and Katherine Ludwig, *Humility Is the New Smart:
> Rethinking Human Excellence in the Smart Machine Age* (Oakland:
> Berrett-Koehler, 2016).

Rob Nielsen, Jennifer A. Marrone, and Holly S. Ferraro, *Leading with Humility* (New York: Routledge, 2014).

Josh Wymore, *Humbler Leadership: How to Enhance Your Effectiveness and Enrich Your Life* (Wayne, IN: Leadership Transformation Lab, 2023).

Merwyn A. Hayes and Michael D. Comer, *Start with Humility: Lessons from America's Quiet CEOs on How to Build Trust and Inspire Followers* (Self-published, 2010).

Marilyn Gist, *The Extraordinary Power of Leader Humility: Thriving Organizations, Great Results* (Oakland: Berrett-Koehler, 2020).

For the more academically inclined, these two journal articles by academics (the first one being a meta-analysis) provide a comprehensive overview of current academic literature on humble leadership:

Y. Luo, Z. Zhang, Q. Chen, K. Zhang, Y. Wang, and J. Peng (2022), "Humble Leadership and Its Outcomes: A Meta-Analysis," *Frontiers Psychology*, 13:980322. https://doi.org/10.3389/fpsyg.2022.980322.

T. K. Kelemen, S. H. Matthews, M. J. Matthews, and S. E. Henry, "Humble Leadership: A Review and Synthesis of Leader Expressed Humility," *Journal of Organizational Behavior*, 2022, 1–23. https://doi.org/10.1002/job.2608.

2    Robert C. Roberts and W. Scott Cleveland, "Humility from a Philosophical Point of View," *Handbook of Humility: Theory, Research and Applications*, edited by Everett L. Worthington Jr., Don E. Davis, and Joshua N. Hook (New York: Routledge, 2017), p. 38.

3    Steven L. Porter, Anantanand Rambachan, Abraham Vélez de Cea, Dani Rabinowitz, Stephen Pardue, and Sherman Jackson, "Religious Perspectives on Humility," *Handbook of Humility: Theory, Research and Applications*, edited by Everett L. Worthington Jr., Don E. Davis, and Joshua N. Hook (New York: Routledge, 2017), p. 46.

4    Jim Collins, *Good to Great: Why Some Companies Make the Leap and Others Don't* (New York: HarperCollins, 2001), 20.

5    Angela S. Wallace, Chia-Yen (Chad) Chiu, and Bradley P. Owens, "Organizational Humility and the Better Functioning Business, Nonprofit and Religious Organization," *Handbook of Humility: Theory, Research and Applications*, ed. Everett L. Worthington Jr., Don E. Davis, and Joshua N. Hook (New York: Routledge, 2017), p. 249.

6    Schein and Schein, *Humble Leadership*.

7    Kenneth H. Blanchard, Patricia Zigarmi, and Drea Zigarmi, *Leadership and the One Minute Manager: Increasing Effectiveness through Situational Leadership* (New York: William Morrow, 1985).

8    Collins, *Good to Great*, p. 20.

9    Clarence Haynes, "Oprah Winfrey: All the Ways the First Black Female Billionaire Has Made History," *Biography.com*, January 29, 2021, https://www.biography.com/news/oprah-winfrey-achievements; Amy C. Edmondson and Tomas Chamorro-Premuzic, "Today's Leaders Need Vulnerability, Not Bravado," *Harvard Business Review*, Oct. 19, 2020, https://hbr.org/2020/10/todays-leaders-need-vulnerability-not-bravado; https://en.wikipedia.org/wiki/Oprah_Winfrey.

10   Sam Walker, *The Captain Class: A New Theory of Leadership* (New York: Random House, 2018).

11   Ibid., pp. 143-145.

12   Bradley P. Owens, Michael D. Johnson, and Terence R. Mitchell, "Expressed Humility in Organizations: Implications for Performance, Teams, and Leadership," *Organization Science*, 2013, 24(5):1517-1538, http://dx.doi.org/10.1287/orsc.1120.079.

## Chapter 2

1    General Stanley McChrystal (with Tantum Collins, David Silvermann, and Chris Fussell), *Team of Teams: New Rules of Engagement for a Complex World* (New York: Portfolio, 2015).

2    Ibid., p. 228.

3    Ibid., p. 218.

4    Ibid., p. 8.

5   Built In., "50 Diversity in the Workplace Statistics to Know," March 28, 2023. https://builtin.com/diversity-inclusion/diversity-in-the-workplace-statistics; Associated Press, "Census Data: US Is Diversifying, White Population Shrinking," August 13, 2021. https://apnews.com/article/race-and-ethnicity-census-2020-7264a653037e38df7ba67d3a324fc90d.

6   Henrik Bresman and Amy Edmondson, "Research: To Excel, Diverse Teams Need Psychological Safety," *Harvard Business Review*, 17, March 2022, https://hbr.org/2022/03/research-to-excel-diverse-teams-need-psychological-safety.

7   Rob Cross, Reb Rebele, and Adam Grant, "Collaborative Overload: Too Much Teamwork Exhausts Employees and Saps Productivity. Here's How to Avoid It," *Harvard Business Review*, January–February 2016, https://hbr.org/2016/01/collaborative-overload.

8   Amy Edmondson, *The Fearless Organization: Creating Psychological Safety in the Workplace for Learning, Innovation and Growth* (Hoboken, NJ: Wiley, 2017), p. xiv.

9   McChrystal, *Team of Teams*, p. 25. Used with permission from the publisher.

10  Stanley McChrystal. "Listen, Learn . . . Then Lead." TED Talk. 2011. https://www.ted.com/talks/stanley_mcchrystal_listen_learn_then_lead.

11  Luo, Zhang, Chen, Zhang, Wang, and Peng, "Humble Leadership and Its Outcomes: A Meta-Analysis"; C. Ma, C.-H. Wu, (G) Z. X. Chen, X. Jiang, and W. Wei (2020), "Why and When Leader Humility Promotes Constructive Voice: A Crossover of Energy Perspective," *Personnel Review*, Vol. 49 No. 5, pp. 1157–1175, https://doi.org/10.1108/PR-02-2019-0049; X. Li, J. Xue, and J. Liu, (2021), "Linking Leader Humility to Employee Creative Performance: Work Engagement as a Mediator," *Social Behavior and Personality. An International Journal*, vol 49, No. 6: 1–7, doi: 10.2224/sbp.10358.

12  Owens, Johnson, and Mitchell, "Expressed Humility in Organizations: Implications for Performance, Teams, and Leadership."

13  T. K. Kelemen, S. H. Matthews, M. J. Matthews, M. J., and S. E. Henry, "Humble Leadership: A Review and Synthesis of Leader Expressed Humility," *Journal of Organizational Behavior*, 2022, 1–23, https://doi.org/10.1002/job.2608.

14  A. Y. Ou, D. A. Waldman, and S. J. Peterson (2018), "Do Humble CEOs Matter? An Examination of CEO Humility and Firm Outcomes," *Journal of Management*, 44(3), 1147–1173, https://doi.org/10.1177/0149206315604187.

15　Edmondson, *The Fearless Organization*, p. 206.

16　L. David Marquet, *Turn the Ship Around!* (New York: Portfolio, 2012).

17　Ibid., p. 82.

18　Ibid., p. 66.

19　Ibid., pp. 202–203.

20　Ryan Holiday, "How Ego Almost Destroyed Steve Jobs' Career," *Fortune.com*, June 14, 2016, https://fortune.com/2016/06/14/ego-steve-jobs/.

21　CBS News (courtesy John Gau Productions), Steve Jobs interview, 2011, https://www.youtube.com/watch?v=kBlc4UX9vZI.

# SHIFT I
## Chapter 3

1　Self-awareness is a leadership imperative, as this selection of articles shows:

> D. Scott Ridley, Paul A. Schultz, Robert S. Glanz, and Claire E. Weinstein, "Self-Regulated Learning: The Interactive Influence of Metacognitive Awareness and Goal-Setting," *The Journal of Experimental Education*, 60:4 (Summer 1992), 293–306, https://www.jstor.org/stable/20152338?seq=1#page_scan_tab_contents.
>
> Clive Fletcher and Caroline Bailey, "Assessing Self-Awareness: Some Issues and Methods," *Journal of Managerial Psychology*, 18:5 (August 1, 2003), 395–404, https://doi.org/10.1108/02683940310484008.
>
> Anna Sutton, Helen M. Williams, and Christopher W. Allinson, "A Longitudinal, Mixed Method Evaluation of Self-Awareness Training in the Workplace," *European Journal of Training and Development*, 39:7 (August 3, 2015), 610–27, https://doi.org/10.1108/EJTD-04-2015-0031.
>
> Bernard M. Bass and Francis J. Yammarino, "Congruence of Self and Others' Leadership Ratings of Naval Officers for Understanding Successful Performance," *Applied Psychology: An International Review*, 40:4 (October 1991), 437–54, https://doi.org/10.1111/j.1464-0597.1991.tb01002.x.

Atuma Okpara and Agwu M. Edwin, "Self-Awareness and Organizational Performance in the Nigerian Banking Sector," *European Journal of Research and Reflection in Management Sciences*, 3:1 (2015), 53–70, https://www.idpublications.org/wp-content/uploads/2014/12/Self-Awareness-and-Organizational-performance-Full-Paper.pdf.

2   Wikipedia, "Johari Window," November 24, 2014. https://en.wikipedia.org/wiki/Johari_window.

3   Marshall Goldsmith and Howard Morgan, "Leadership Is a Contact Sport: The Follow-Up Factor in Management Development," *Strategy and Business*, Fall 2004, Issue 36, https://www.strategy-business.com/article/04307.

4   Adapted from Deborah Grayson Riegel, "How to Encourage Your Team to Give You Honest Feedback," *Harvard Business Review*, October 28, 2022, https://hbr.org/2022/10/how-to-encourage-your-team-to-give-you-honest-feedback?utm_medium=email&utm_source=newsletter_weekly&utm_campaign=weeklyhotlist_activesubs&utm_content=signinnudge&deliveryName=DM227027.

5   Joseph Folkman, "Top Ranked Leaders Know This Secret: Ask for Feedback," *Forbes.com*, Jan. 8, 2015, https://www.forbes.com/sites/joefolkman/2015/01/08/top-ranked-leaders-know-this-secret-ask-for-feedback/?sh=4ba700b03195.

## Chapter 4

1   Graham Jones, "How the Best of the Best Get Better and Better," *Harvard Business Review*, June 2008, https://hbr.org/2008/06/how-the-best-of-the-best-get-better-and-better.

2   Jeremiah Brown, *The 4 Year Olympian: From First Stroke to Olympic Medalist* (Toronto: Dundurn, 2018).

3   Greg McKeown, *Essentialism: Disciplined Pursuit of Less* (New York: Crown, 2014), p. 20.

4   Ibid., p. 17.

5   Ibid., p. 5.

6   Jennifer Herrity, "How to Write a Personal Mission Statement (40 Examples)," Indeed.com, September 30, 2002, https://www.indeed.com/career-advice/career-development/personal-mission-statement-examples.

7    This blog article provides an excellent overview of some of the best books written on goal setting: Kelly Miller. "15 Best Goal Setting Books to Read." PositivePsychology.com, July 4, 2019. https://positivepsychology.com/goal-setting-books/.

8    Remy Blumenfeld, "Toxic Friendships and How to End Them," *Forbes.com*, July 22, 2019, https://www.forbes.com/sites/remyblumenfeld/2019/07/22/how-to-end-a-toxic-friendship/?sh=4167554856b9.

9    Bronnie Ware, *Top Five Regrets of the Dying: A Life Transformed by the Dearly Departing* (Carlsbad, CA: Hay House, 2019), pp. 44–86.

## Chapter 5

1    Karen Reivich, Martin E. P. Seligman, and Sharon McBride, "Master Resilience Training in the US Army," *American Psychologist* 66 (1): pp. 25–34, January 2011, https://ppc.sas.upenn.edu/sites/default/files/mrtinarmyjan2011.pdf.

2    Andrew M. Luks, Thomas H. Robertson, and Erik R. Swenson, "An Ultracyclist with Pulmonary Edema during the Bicycle Race Across America," *Medicine & Science in Sports & Exercise* 39(1):p 8-12, January 2007, DOI: 10.1249/01.mss.0000235885.79110.79.

3    Adapted from Joshua D. Margolis and Paul Stoltz, "How to Bounce Back from Adversity," *Harvard Business Review*, January–February, 2010, https://hbr.org/2010/01/how-to-bounce-back-from-adversity.

4    Carol S. Dweck, *Mindset: The New Psychology of Success* (New York: Ballantine, 2016).

5    Benjamin Hardy, "23 Michael Jordan Quotes That Will Immediately Boost Your Confidence," Inc.com, April 5, 2015, https://www.inc.com/benjamin-p-hardy/23-michael-jordan-quotes-that-will-immediately-boost-your-confidence.html.

# SHIFT II
## Chapter 6

1    Glassdoor Team, "New Survey: Company Mission & Culture Matter More Than Salary," July 11, 2019, https://www.glassdoor.co.uk/blog/mission-culture-survey/.

2   Claire Hastwell, "The Six Elements of Great Company Culture," Greatplacetowork. com, August 19, 2021, https://www.greatplacetowork.com/resources/ blog/6-elements-of-great-company-culture.

3   Adapted from Schein and Schein, *Humble Leadership*, p. 13.

4   Schein and Schein, *Humble Leadership*, pp. 18–19.

5   Adapted from Schein and Schein, Humble Leadership, 135 (with permission from publisher).

6   McKinsey and Company, "Culture in the Hybrid Workplace," podcast, July 11, 2021, https://www.mckinsey.com/capabilities/people-and-organizational-performance/ our-insights/culture-in-the-hybrid-workplace.

7   McChrystal, *Team of Teams*, p. 127.

## Chapter 7

1   Kim Scott, *Radical Candor: Be a Kick-Ass Boss without Losing Your Humanity* (New York: St. Martin's Publishing Group, 2019), pp. 10–13.

2   Rasmus Hougaard and Jacqueline Carter (with Marissa Afton and Moses Mohan), *Compassionate Leadership: How to Do Hard Things in a Human Way* (Boston: HBR Press, 2022), pp. 3–4.

3   Oren Harari, *The Leadership Secrets of Colin Powell* (New York: McGraw-Hill, 2002), pp. 255–256.

4   Dale Carnegie, *How to Win Friends & Influence People* (New York: Gallery, 1936), pp. 13–14.

## SHIFT III
### Chapter 8

1   Harvard News, "Former Mass. Governor Deval Patrick on Leadership during Boston Marathon Bombing Response," November 12, 2015. https://www.hsph. harvard.edu/news/features/former-mass-governor-deval-patrick-on-leadership- during-boston-marathon-bombing-response/.

2   Collins, *Good to Great*, pp. 41–64.

3    Helene Cooper, Eric Schmitt, and Julian E. Barnes, "As Russia's Military Stumbles, Its Adversaries Take Note," *New York Times*, March 7, 2022, https://www.nytimes.com/2022/03/07/us/politics/russia-ukraine-military.html.

4    *Harvard Business Review Podcast*, "Former Best Buy CEO Hubert Joly: Empowering Workers to Create 'Magic,'" December 2, 2021, https://hbr.org/2021/12/former-best-buy-ceo-hubert-joly-empowering-workers-to-create-magic.

5    Jamil Zaki, "Don't Let Cynicism Undermine Your Workplace," *Harvard Business Review*, September–October 2022, https://hbr.org/2022/09/dont-let-cynicism-undermine-your-workplace.

6    Donald Sull, James Sull, and James Yoder, "No One Knows Your Strategy, Not Even Your Top Leaders," *MIT Sloan Management Review*, February 12, 2018, https://sloanreview.mit.edu/article/no-one-knows-your-strategy-not-even-your-top-leaders/.

7    Mark Miller, "Building Brand Legacy for the Age of Now: The Ritz-Carlton," *Fastcompany.com*, January 30, 2017, https://www.fastcompany.com/3067506/building-brand-legacy-for-the-age-of-now-the-ritz-carlton.

## Chapter 9

1    Daniel Coyle: *The Culture Code: The Secrets of Highly Successful Groups* (New York: Bantam, 2018), p. 168.

2    Richard Haythornthwaite and Ajay Banga, "The Former and Current Chairs of Mastercard on Executing a Strategic CEO Succession," *Harvard Business Review*, March–April 2021, https://hbr.org/2021/03/the-former-and-current-chairs-of-mastercard-on-executing-a-strategic-ceo-succession.

3    Anthony C. Klotz, Andrea Derler, Carlina Kim, and Manda Winlaw, "The Promise (and Risk) of Boomerang Employees," *Harvard Business Review*, March 15, 2023, https://hbr.org/2023/03/the-promise-and-risk-of-boomerang-employees?utm_medium=email&utm_source=newsletter_daily&utm_campaign=dailyalert_actsubs&utm_content=signinnudge&deliveryName=DM261157.

4    Ryan Bonnici, "Why I Encourage My Best Employees to Consider Outside Job Offers," *Harvard Business Review*, September 2018, https://rb.gy/eatis.

# SHIFT IV

## Chapter 10

1   Brené Brown: *Dare to Lead: Brave Work. Tough Conversations. Whole Hearts* (New York: Random House, 2018), p. 79.

2   Adam Lashinsky, "How Microsoft CEO Satya Nadella Fueled a Humble Comeback," *Fortune.com*, January 15, 2019, https://fortune.com/2019/01/15/microsoft-comeback-satya-nadella-humble/.

3   Amy Edmondson and Tomas Chamorro-Premuzic, "Today's Leaders Need Vulnerability, Not Bravado," *Harvard Business Review*, October 19, 2020, https://hbr.org/2020/10/todays-leaders-need-vulnerability-not-bravado; Clarence Haynes, "Oprah Winfrey: All the Ways the First Black Female Billionaire Has Made History," Biography.com, January 29, 2021, https://www.biography.com/news/oprah-winfrey-achievements.

4   Nick Perry, "New Zealand's Jacinda Ardern, an Icon to Many, to Step Down," APnews.com, January 19, 2023, https://apnews.com/article/politics-new-zealand-government-covid-jacinda-ardern-0e6d8eedd96f94aab07eeb0c37164591.

5   Jeffrey Cohn and U. Srinivasa Rangan, "Why CEOs Should Model Vulnerability," *Harvard Business Review*, May 11, 2020, https://hbr.org/2020/05/why-ceos-should-model-vulnerability.

6   Coyle, *The Culture Code*, pp. 104–105.

7   Kaissi, *Humbitious*, p. 144.

8   Coyle, *The Culture Code*, pp. 140–141.

9   Ibid., p. 145.

10  Amy Edmondson and Per Hugander, "4 Steps to Boost Psychological Safety at Your Workplace," *Harvard Business Review*, June 22, 2021, https://hbr.org/2021/06/4-steps-to-boost-psychological-safety-at-your-workplace.

## Chapter 11

1   Buffer. "Transparent Salaries," n.d. https://buffer.com/salaries.

2  Buffer (Resources), "How We Decide What To Pay Our Team: Our Salary Formula and Compensation Philosophy," March 24, 2021. https://buffer.com/resources/compensation-philosophy; Sam Forsdick, "Buffer's Salary Policy Takes Transparency to Another Level," *Rancoteur.net*, May 20, 2022, https://www.raconteur.net/against-the-grain/buffer-transparent-salary-pay/.

3  Catherine Clifford, "Whole Foods CEO John Mackey: Store Managers Could Be Making 'Well Over $100,000,' without a College Degree," CNBC.com, November 5, 2020, https://www.cnbc.com/2020/11/05/ceo-john-mackey-on-how-much-you-can-make-working-at-whole-foods.html.

4  Brown, *Dare to Lead*, p. 111.

5  Gene Hammett, "3 Steps Ray Dalio Uses Radical Transparency to Build a Billion-Dollar Company," *Inc*, May 23, 2018, https://www.inc.com/gene-hammett/3-steps-ray-dalio-uses-radical-transparency-to-build-a-billion-dollar-company.html#:~:text=Ray%20Dalio%20on%20Radical%20Transparency&text=%22I%20want%20independent%20thinkers%20who,radical%20truth%20and%20radical%20transparency.

6  Richard Feloni, "Employees at the World's Largest Hedge Fund Use iPads to Rate Each Other's Performance in Real Time—See How It Works," *Businessinsider.com*, September 6, 2017, https://www.businessinsider.com/bridgewater-ray-dalio-radical-transparency-app-dots-2017-9.

7  Ray Dalio, "How to Build a Company Where the Best Ideas Win." TED Talk, 2017. https://www.ted.com/talks/ray_dalio_how_to_build_a_company_where_the_best_ideas_win.

8  Bess Levine, "Hedge-Fund Guru Ray Dalio Is Bringing His Cult to Silicon Valley," *Vanityfair.com*, September 18, 2017, https://www.vanityfair.com/news/2017/09/ray-dalio-is-bringing-his-cult-to-silicon-valley; https://www.nytimes.com/2017/09/08/business/dealbook/bridgewaters-ray-dalio-spreads-his-gospel-of-radical-transparency.html.

9  Nicholas Gordon, "Coinbase Reportedly Wants Staff to Rate Each Other Using an App, Adopting a Controversial Management Principle Called 'Radical Transparency,'" *Fortune.com*, May 24, 2022, https://fortune.com/2022/05/24/coinbase-dot-collector-app-employee-radical-transparency-bridgewater-ray-dalio/~.

10   Warren Berger: *The Book of Beautiful Question: The Powerful Questions That Will Help You Decide, Create, Connect, and Lead* (New York: Bloomsbury, 2018), p. 30.

11   Sprout Data Report, "#BrandsGetReal: Social Media & the Evolution of Transparency," Sproutsocial.com, April 9, 2018, https://sproutsocial.com/insights/data/social-media-transparency/.

12   Everlane. "Everlane," n.d. https://www.everlane.com.

13   Patagonia. "Environmental Responsibility - Patagonia," n.d. https://www.patagonia.com/environmental-responsibility-materials/.

14   Jeffrey Cohn and U. Srinivasa Rangan, "Why CEOs Should Model Vulnerability," *Harvard Business Review*, May 11, 2020, https://hbr.org/2020/05/why-ceos-should-model-vulnerability.

15   Ibid.

## SHIFT V

1   Roderick I. Swaab, Michael Schaerer, Erich M. Anicich, Richard Ronay, and Adam D. Galinsky (2014), "The Too-Much-Talent Effect: Team Interdependence Determines When More Talent Is Too Much or Not Enough," *Psychological Science*, 25(8), 1581–1591. https://doi.org/10.1177/0956797614537280.

## *Chapter 12*

1   Ideacast, "Creating Psychological Safety in the Workplace," *Harvard Business Review* podcast. January 22, 2019. https://hbr.org/podcast/2019/01/creating-psychological-safety-in-the-workplace.

2   Amy Gallo, "What Is Psychological Safety?," *Harvard Business Review*, February 15, 2023, https://hbr.org/2023/02/what-is-psychological-safety.

3   Coyle, *The Culture Code*, p. xvi.

4   Wujec, Tom. "Build a Tower, Build a Team." TED Talk, 2010. https://www.ted.com/talks/tom_wujec_build_a_tower_build_a_team.

5   YouTube. "Peter Skillman Marshmallow Design Challenge," January 27, 2014. https://www.youtube.com/watch?v=1p5sBzMtB3Q.

6   Coyle, *The Culture Code*, p. xviii.

7    Google, "Five Keys to a Successful Google Team," November 17, 2015, https://rework.withgoogle.com/blog/five-keys-to-a-successful-google-team.

8    Edmondson, *The Fearless Organization*, pp. 29–49.

9    Alan Murray and David Meyer, "Putting the Postpandemic Design Process into Context," *Fortune.com*, May 2, 2022, https://fortune.com/2022/05/02/putting-the-postpandemic-design-process-into-context-gratton-ceo-daily/.

10   Natalie Kitroeff and David Gelles, "Claims of Shoddy Production Draw Scrutiny to a Second Boeing Jet," *New York Times*, April 20, 2019, https://www.nytimes.com/2019/04/20/business/boeing-dreamliner-production-problems.html.

11   Julie Johnsson and Ryan Beene, "Internal Boeing Messages Say 737 Max 'Designed by Clowns,'" Bloomberg.com, January 9, 2020, https://www.bloomberg.com/news/articles/2020-01-10/-incredibly-damning-boeing-messages-show-employee-unease-on-max; Amy Edmondson, "Boeing and the Importance of Encouraging Employees to Speak Up," *Harvard Business Review*, May 1, 2019, https://hbr.org/2019/05/boeing-and-the-importance-of-encouraging-employees-to-speak-up; Dominic Gates and Mike Baker, "Engineers Say Boeing Pushed to Limit Safety Testing in Race to Certify Planes Including 737 Max," *Seattletimes.com*, May 5, 2019, https://www.seattletimes.com/business/boeing-aerospace/engineers-say-boeing-pushed-to-limit-safety-testing-in-race-to-certify-planes-including-737-max/.

12   Wikipedia, "Volkswagen Emissions Scandal," May 23, 2016. https://en.wikipedia.org/wiki/Volkswagen_emissions_scandal.

13   Wikipedia, "Wells Fargo Cross-Selling Scandal," December 3, 2020. https://en.wikipedia.org/wiki/Wells_Fargo_cross-selling_scandal.

14   Schein and Schein, *Humble Leadership*, p. 8.

15   Edmondson and Hugander, "4 Steps to Boost Psychological Safety at Your Workplace."

16   Edmondson, *The Fearless Organization*, p. 20.

## Chapter 13

1    Scott, *Radical Candor*, p. 166.

2    Edmondson, *The Fearless Organization*, p. 161.

3    Ibid., pp. 163, 180. Adapted with permission from the publisher.

4    Marilyn Gist, *The Extraordinary Power of Leader Humility: Thriving Organization-Great Results* (Oakland: Berrett-Koehler, 2020), p. 117

5    Bryce G. Hoffman, *American Icon: Alan Mulally and the Fight to Save Ford Motor Company* (New York: Crown, 2012), p. 124.

6    Mark Lister, "The Three Levels of Listening," Co-Active Training Institute, November 30, 2022, https://coactive.com/blog/levels-of-listening/.

7    McKinsey and Company, "Psychological Safety and the Critical Role of Leadership Development—Survey," February 11, 2021, https://www.mckinsey.com/capabilities/people-and-organizational-performance/our-insights/psychological-safety-and-the-critical-role-of-leadership-development.

8    Kevin M. Kniffin, Brian Wansink, Carol M. Devine, and Jeffery Sobal, "Eating Together at the Firehouse: How Workplace Commensality Relates to the Performance of Firefighters," *Human Performance*, Volume 28, 2015—Issue 4, pp. 281–306, https://doi.org/10.1080/08959285.2015.1021049.

9    Coyle, *The Culture Code*, p. 82.

10   Aman Kidwai, "Taco Bell Has a Unique Strategy to Improve Its Frontline Experience: Make Corporate Employees Work Restaurant Shifts," *Fortune.com*, August 9, 2022, https://fortune.com/2022/08/09/taco-bell-unique-strategy-to-improve-frontline-work-experience-make-corporate-employees-work-restaurant-shifts/?utm_source=Iterable&utm_medium=email&utm_campaign=fortunedaily&tpcc=nlfortunedaily.

11   Schein and Schein, *Humble Leadership*, p. 53.

12   First Round Review, "The Founder's Guide to Discipline: Lessons from Front's Mathilde Collin," https://review.firstround.com/the-founders-guide-to-discipline-lessons-from-fronts-mathilde-collin#disciplined-team-building-highlight-impact-and-stage-an-office-musical.

# ABOUT THE AUTHOR

**URS KOENIG** is a former United Nations military peacekeeper and NATO military peacekeeping commander, a highly accomplished ultra-endurance champion, a widely published professor, and a seasoned executive coach and keynote speaker with more than three decades of experience helping hundreds of leaders and dozens of executive teams unlock new levels of achievement across four continents.

He is the founder of the Radical Humility Leadership Institute and speaks frequently on the topic of leadership to corporations and associations across the globe. His message of Radical Humility in leadership has inspired teams from across the spectrum, including Amazon, Starbucks, the Society for Human Resource Management, Vistage, the University of Melbourne, and Microsoft.

He holds a PhD in geography and a master of science from the University of Zürich, Switzerland, and an MBA from the Australian Graduate School of Management.

He lives with his two sons in Seattle, Washington.

 @URSKOENIG     @KOENIGURS     URS KOENIG